30

SEASONS AT VILLA PARK

1974-75 TO 2003-04

David Powter

SOCCER BOOKS
LIMITED

CONTENTS

British Library Cataloguing in Publication Data
A catalogue record for this book is available from the British Library

ISBN 1-86223-096-X

Printed by The Cromwell Press

ASTON VILLA – 30 SEASONS 1974-75 TO 2003-2004

INTRODUCTION

Founded in 1874, Football League founder member Aston Villa F.C. is one of the oldest and most famous clubs in English football. All-told the club has won 20 major tropies (seven League titles and 13 cups) and six of these trophies (including the European Cup) were lifted during the 30 years up to the summer of 2004.

Aston Villa struggled during the 1960s although they did win the very first League Cup competition (in 1960-61). They were relegated to the Second Division in 1967 and experienced their first taste of Third Division football three years later. However, they gallantly reached the 1970-71 League Cup final and, under Vic Crowe's stewardship, lifted the Third Division title in 1971-72. They almost celebrated another promotion 12 months later when they finished third in the second-flight. They lost their way somewhat in 1973-74, finishing only 14th; but promotion and another major trophy was to be just around the corner!

1974-1975 SEASON

Vic Crowe was replaced by Ron Saunders during the summer of 1974 and the fans were optimistic that Villa would quickly regain their top-flight status. The Holte End certainly could not complain and more than got their money's worth during 1974-75. Aston Villa survived a shaky patch at the end of 1974 (when they lost six out of ten fixtures) to finish as the runners-up, three points behind Manchester United.

Aston Villa clinched promotion by taking full points from the last eight fixtures. 20-goal Brian Little pipped Ray Graydon by one goal to be the top scorer, while Chico Hamilton contributed 10 goals.

Villa defeated First Division Sheffield United in the F.A. Cup before exiting at Ipswich in the fifth round. However, the real cup glory came in the League Cup. Villa shocked First Division Everton by winning 3-0 at Goodison Park in the second round and then navigated a course past four lower Division sides to meet fellow Second Division promotion hunters Norwich City in the final at Wembley.

A 100,000 crowd witnessed a very tight final, which was settled by just one second half goal. The scorer was Graydon, who followed up to net the rebound after the Norwich goalkeeper Kevin Keelan had pushed his penalty onto the inside of a post. It was Aston Villa's first major trophy success since they won the same competition 14 years earlier.

Graydon's team-mates on the day that Aston Villa lifted the League Cup in 1975 were: goalie Jim Cumbes, John Robson, Charlie Aitken, Ian Ross, Chris Nicholl, Bob McDonald, Keith Leonard, Frank Carrodus, Little and Hamilton.

For his side's exploits in 1974-75, Saunders became the first Aston Villa boss to be voted 'Manager of the Year'.

1975-1976 SEASON

The League Cup success presented Villa with their first opportunity of European football and two first round UEFA Cup ties with Antwerp. However, it was not a happy baptism, the Belgians won both games (5-1 on aggregate).

Villa were inconsistent in the League in 1975-76. They failed to secure an away victory, but steered clear of the relegation zone, in 16th place, on the back of their home form which gained them all but nine of their 39 points. New signing Andy Gray (ex-Dundee United) contributed 10 goals, two fewer than the leading scorer Ray Graydon. Among the men who played their last games for Villa in 1975-76 was defender Charlie Aitken. The Scot made a club record 561 League appearances (scoring 13 goals).

Aston Villa's hold on the League Cup slipped at the third round stage, when they lost 2-1 to Manchester United. There was little joy in the F.A. Cup either, with Second Division Southampton triumphing in extra-time of a third round replay.

1976-1977 SEASON

Aston Villa were more consistent in 1976-77 and were always in the top half of the table. They finished in an excellent fourth place. Andy Gray was the top scorer (with 25 goals), Brian Little netted 14 times and John Deehan contributed 13 goals. Ron Saunders was lucky to have such a settled team, with 12 men making 27 or more appearances. One man who made his last appearance for Villa in 1976-77 was centre-half Chris Nicholl, who joined Southampton, after making 210 League appearances (11 goals) for the Villans.

1976-77 was another marvellous cup season for Aston Villa. They won through to the F.A. Cup quarter-final without conceding a goal; but were then defeated by Manchester United at Old Trafford. However, a few weeks later, on the same ground, Villa lifted the League Cup for the second time in three seasons when they defeated

Everton in the second replay of the Final. There were no goals at Wembley, and the Hillsborough replay ended 1-1, with Villa benefiting from an own goal.

Everton took the lead in the third match at Old Trafford; but first Nicholl and then Brian Little scored for the Villans. Everton equalised to send the match into extra-time and, with only 60 seconds remaining, Little netted his second to send the trophy back to Villa Park.

The men that participated in the three League Cup Final encounters with Everton in 1976-77 were: goalkeeper John Burridge, John Gidman, John Robson, Leighton Phillips, Dennis Mortimer, Deehan, Nicholl, Little, Gray, Alex Cropley, Frank Carrodus, Ray Graydon, Gordon Cowans and Gordon Smith. The first eight named men started all three games.

1977-1978 SEASON

The Villans had their first success against European opposition in 1977-78, when they defeated Fenerbahce (home and away) in the UEFA Cup. They followed up by disposing of Gornik Zabrze and Athletic Bilbao to earn two quarter-final ties with Barcelona. After being held 2-2 at home, Villa went down gallantly, 2-1, in front 90,000 at the Nou Camp.

Aston Villa made a sluggish start to their League campaign and for much of the 1977-78 season oscillated between eighth and 11th position in the table. They eventually finished eighth, after winning five of their last six fixtures. 13-goal Andy Gray was the top scorer, bagging two more than John Deehan.

Everton exacted some revenge for the previous season's League Cup final defeat by beating the Villans 4-1 at Goodison Park in an F.A. Cup tie. Nottingham Forest had earlier proved too good for Villa in the fourth round of the League Cup.

1978-1979 SEASON

Aston Villa made a promising start to 1978-79, winning three of their first five fixtures, including matches at White Hart Lane and Portman Road. They were in the top half of the table for the greater part of the campaign and again finished eighth, ending on a high note by winning 3-2 at Maine Road. John Deehan was the main marksman, netting nine times – two more than John Gregory and Gary Shelton.

There was little joy in the cups. Second Division Luton Town ended their League

Cup run in the fourth round, while Nottingham Forest beat them 2-0 in a third round F.A. Cup tie at the City Ground.

1979-1980 SEASON

Aston Villa made a muddled start to 1979-80 and had slipped into the relegation zone by the end of September. However, an 11-game unbeaten run gave them a boost and they gradually worked their way into the top five before end of season defeats at the top two sides (Liverpool and Manchester United) meant that they had to settle for a seventh place finish.

Gary Shaw was the leading scorer (with nine), while the injury-hit Brian Little played in his 247th and last League game (60 goals) for the Villans in 1979-80.

Another 4-1 defeat at Goodison Park signalled the end of Villa's League Cup run. In the F.A. Cup, they overcame three lower division outfits to earn a quarter-final tie at West Ham United. A penalty in the second half was all that divided the teams, but it was the Second Division side who triumphed. West Ham went on to lift the cup.

1980-1981 SEASON

The signing of striker Peter Withe (from Newcastle United), in the summer of 1980, proved to be a masterstroke by Ron Saunders (who for the second time was voted 'Manager of the Season'). In his first campaign in claret & blue, Withe netted 20 League goals to be the First Division's leading scorer. He also set up many more goals for his colleagues as Aston Villa clinched their first Football League championship for seventy years. Withe collected his first three England caps later in the season on the back of a string of magnificent performances for his club.

A 12-match unbeaten run in the autumn had sent Villa on their way and seven consecutive victories in January and February stoked up the momentum. A late spurt took the Villans past long time leaders Ipswich Town. A final day reverse at Highbury did not prove costly as Ipswich also slipped up at Middlesbrough. The final margin of points over the runners-up was four, with Ipswich also losing their game in hand.

Villa were exceedingly lucky with injuries in 1980-81 and Saunders only needed to call on 14 players. Seven men were ever-present. They were goalkeeper Jimmy Rimmer, Kenny Swain, Ken McNaught, Dennis Mortimer, Des Bremner, Gordon Cowans and 10-goal Tony Morley. Gary Shaw was the second highest scorer (with 18) while Allan Evans, Gary Williams, Colin Gibson, Eamonn Deacy and David Geddis also made valuable contributions.

Third round defeats to Ipswich and Second Division Cambridge United, in the F.A. Cup and League Cup, respectively, only enabled the Villans to focus more fully on their principal target in 1980-81.

1981-1982 SEASON

An opening day home defeat by newly promoted Notts County was an early pointer to Villa's prospects of retaining the title. A club record sequence of six successive draws and seven defeats in ten fixtures at the end of the first half of the season effectively killed off those ambitions. Meanwhile, they reached the European Cup quarter-final by beating Valur and then edging out Dynamo Berlin on away goals; but had slipped out of the League Cup to West Bromwich Albion in a quarter-final on their own ground.

Villa Park was rocked by the surprise resignation of Ron Saunders on 9th February. Saunders, who soon afterwards became the Birmingham City manager, was in dispute with his board. He had been 'Manager of the Year' twice while at Villa Park. His assistant Tony Barton took the reins on a temporary basis and steered Villa into the European Cup Final, courtesy of goalless draws at Dynamo Kiev and Anderlecht. Villa won the home legs 2-0 and 1-0, respectively.

By the time of the Final in Rotterdam, Villa had finished their League campaign in 11th place (with Peter Withe top scoring with 10 goals), gone out of the F.A. Cup at Tottenham and Barton had earned himself the permanent post as manager. The Final was a marvellous triumph for the Villans as Bayern Munich's big names were beaten by a single second half goal by Withe. However, the real hero was substitute goalkeeper Nigel Spink (in only his second game), who replaced the injured Jimmy Rimmer after just eight minutes.

The other men who helped Aston Villa become only the fourth English club to lift the European Cup were: Kenny Swain, Gary Williams, Allan Evans, Ken McNaught, Dennis Mortimer, Des Bremner, Gary Shaw, Gordon Cowans and Tony Morley.

RON SAUNDERS

Reign: 1974-82
Honours: Football League champions, League Cup & Division Two champions
Highest League finish: Champions in 1980-81
Best F.A. Cup Run: Quarter-finals in 1976-77 and 1979-80
Best League Cup Run: Winners in 1974-75
Best European Run: European Cup Semi-final in 1981-82

1982-1983 SEASON

The campaign started disastrously with three straight League defeats (including a 5-0 reverse at Goodison Park) and two reverses against Notts County. However, Villa won 10 of the next 14 League fixtures to lift themselves into third place. A five game winless run knocked them backwards, but Tony Barton's side plugged on to finish in sixth place despite the distractions of other competitions. 17-goal Gary Shaw was the main marksman, Peter Withe netted 16 times and Gordon Cowans contributed 10 goals.

Jimmy Rimmer (229 League appearances) and central defender Ken McNaught (207 League appearances – 8 goals) played their last games for the Villans in 1982-83.

Aston Villa's grip on the European Cup loosened after Juventus netted a first minute goal against them in the quarter-final first leg at Villa Park. The Italians went on to take a 2-1 lead to Turin. Ten days later, in a different quarter-final, Villa's F.A. Cup dreams evaporated when Arsenal triumphed 2-0 at Highbury. Predictably Juventus allowed them no way back in the second leg and Barton's men had exited two cups in the space of five days.

1983-1984 SEASON

After winning their opening two 1983-84 fixtures, Villa lost form and experienced a period of struggle. They were thumped 6-2 on their own pitch by Arsenal at the end of October and, during the following month, went down 5-2 at Notts County. However, seven points were accumulated from three games in between and a similar tally was gained from the three games afterwards. Villa were dogged by inconsistency all season and could do no better than finish tenth. Peter Withe was the leading scorer (with 16), netting twice as many as the next highest scorer Mark Walters.

Aston Villa defeated Portsmouth, Manchester City, West Bromwich Albion and Norwich City en route to two League Cup semi-final clashes with Everton. The Toffeemen held a two goal advantage after the first leg and although substitute Paul Rideout netted for Tony Barton's side at Villa Park it was not enough to secure another trip to the Twin Towers. The Villans exited the F.A. Cup at Norwich, in a third round replay.

TONY BARTON

Reign: 1982-84
Honours: European Cup
Highest League finish: 6th in 1982-83
Best F.A. Cup Run: Quarter-final in 1982-83
Best League Cup Run: Semi-final in 1983-84
Best European Run: European Cup Winners in 1981-82

1984-1985 SEASON

After two full campaigns at the helm, Tony Barton was sacked and replaced by Shrewsbury Town boss Graham Turner during the summer of 1984. Turner's reign started well, with two victories, but Villa gradually drifted into the middle of the pack with a seven match winless sequence. Four consecutive successes in January and February lifted them into the top half and they finished in tenth spot. Paul Rideout was the top scorer (with 14), while Peter Withe netted 12 times and Mark Walters scored 10 goals. Midfielder Dennis Mortimer made his 317th and last League appearance (31 goals) for the club in 1984-85.

Turner's side exited both cups at the third round stage. They lost 1-0 at Queen's Park Rangers in the League Cup and were beaten 3-0 at Anfield in the F.A. Cup.

1985-1986 SEASON

Aston Villa made a poor start to the 1985-86 campaign, taking just one point one from their first three games. They found their form with a seven match unbeaten run; but then slithered into a horrendous patch, winning only two of the next 21 fixtures. Five victories from the last 11 fixtures just saved them from relegation (by three points), in 16th place. Mark Walters and Simon Stainrod (in his first season at the club) were the joint top scorers with 10 goals apiece.

Villa's best form in 1985-86 was reserved for the League Cup, where they netted 25 times (Stainrod bagging nine of them). They side-stepped Exeter City, Leeds United, West Bromwich Albion and Arsenal to reach the last four. However, they were then defeated by the eventual winners Oxford United, 4-3 on aggregate. Second Division Millwall proved too good for the Villans in the fourth round of the F.A. Cup.

1986-1987 SEASON

Graham Turner lost his job at Villa Park after a terrible start to the 1986-87 campaign. After six games, his side sat next to bottom in the table after suffering five defeats. The day before he was sacked the first team lost 6-0 at Nottingham Forest, while the reserves were beaten 7-0 at home by Manchester United.

Former Celtic defender Billy McNeill became the new man at the helm. There was a hint of better days to come as Villa won four games out of five in October and early November; but they then embarked on a dreadful run that lasted for the remainder of the season. Just three more victories were recorded in 29 games (including a club record sequence of 12 fixtures without a win) and Villa slipped into the Second Division in 22nd and bottom place. Simon Stainrod, Garry Thompson and the penalty-taker Allan Evans were the club's joint top scorers with just six goals apiece.

Aston Villa experienced only moderate success in the cups in 1986-87. They were beaten by Southampton in the fourth round of the League Cup and lost an F.A. Cup third round replay at Chelsea.

GRAHAM TURNER

Reign: 1984-86
Honours: None
Highest League finish: 10th in 1984-85
Best F.A. Cup Run: Round 4 in 1985-86
Best League Cup Run: Semi-final in 1985-86

BILLY McNEILL

Reign: 1986-87
Honours: None
Highest League finish: 22nd in 1986-87
Best F.A. Cup Run: Round 3 in 1986-87
Best League Cup Run: Round 4 in 1986-87

1987-1988 SEASON

An inevitable consequence of relegation was Billy McNeill's dismissal after less than one season at the club. His successor was the highly-respected Watford boss Graham Taylor.

The early results in 1987-88 were not particularly promising, with just one win recorded in the first seven games. However, a 12-match unbeaten run lifted Taylor's side into the promotion frame and by the turn of year they were at the head of the table. Seven defeats in 10 games in the last third of the season nearly destroyed their promotion chance; but they rallied again to grab second place by collecting eight points from the last four fixtures. However, it was a close call as an away draw at Swindon on the final day only proved good enough because their two rivals, Middlesbrough and Bradford City, both lost. Villa accumulated a club record 78 points in 1978-88.

One of Taylor's most inspired signings during 1987-88 was David Platt (from Crewe Alexandra), who scored five times in 11 games. Warren Aspinall and Garry Thompson were the joint top goalscorers, with 11 apiece. Goalkeeper Nigel Spink and right-back Kevin Gage were ever-present, while Bernard Gallagher missed just one game and Martin Keown (in his first season following his move from Arsenal) played in all but two fixtures.

The Villans reached the fourth round of both cup competitions. They found Liverpool too strong for them in the F.A. Cup and lost to another First Division outfit Sheffield Wednesday in the League Cup.

1988-1989 SEASON

Despite a five game unbeaten start, 1988-89 largely proved to be a season of hard graft and struggle. At the end of it, the Villans finished one point and one place above the drop in 17th. They drew 1-1 at home to Coventry City on the final day of the season and, for the second time in 12 months, Aston Villa's fate was decided elsewhere. Middlesbrough (who had joined Villa in the top-flight via the play-offs) were yet again involved. If the Ayresome Park outfit had won (rather than lost) at Hillsborough, then Graham Taylor's side would have been relegated in their place.

Villa's main marksman was 14-goal Alan McInally, while the ever-present David Platt chipped in with seven goals to be the club's second highest goalscorer. Allan Evans made his 380th and last League appearance (51 goals) for Villa in 1988-89.

Aston Villa defeated local rivals Birmingham City, Millwall and Ipswich Town en route to a League Cup quarter-final meeting with West Ham United. The match at the Boleyn Ground went the Hammers' way 2-1. The F.A. Cup run was rather shorter, with Wimbledon triumphing at Villa Park in the fourth round.

1989-1990 SEASON

After a mixed start, Aston Villa embarked on a fantastic run of 15 wins from 18 games to take them to the top of the First Division table. However, Graham Taylor's side could not quite last the pace with Liverpool and had to be content with the runners-up berth, nine points adrift of the champions.

Second place was an extremely creditable performance; but with a little more fire-power, Villa (who netted 57 goals) might have snatched the title. David Platt was the highest scorer with 19, ten more than second top scorer Ian Olney. At the other end of the pitch, goalie Nigel Spink, Chris Price, Stuart Gray, Derek Mountfield and Kent Nielsen formed a formidable defensive unit.

Villa's League Cup run was again ended by West Ham, at the Boleyn Ground, while their F.A. Cup run promised more than it delivered. After beating Blackburn Rovers, Port Vale and West Bromwich Albion, they crashed out 3-0 at Second Division Oldham Athletic in the quarter-finals.

1990-1991 SEASON

With Graham Taylor taking control of the England national side, the Villa board showed great imagination in appointing Dr Josef Venglos (the manager of the Czechoslovakian national side) to be the new head coach.

Villa started 1990-91 reasonably well in the League and defeated Banik Ostrava in the first round of the UEFA Cup. The second round draw paired them with Internazionale. Everything went to plan in the first leg as the Villans won 2-0. However, it was a different story at the San Siro, where the Italians won 3-0 with Jürgen Klinsmann netting the first goal.

Dreams of League Cup glory disintegrated at Elland Road, where Leeds beat them 2-1 in a quarter-final. While in the F.A. Cup, Wimbledon defeated them 1-0 in a third round replay.

Aston Villa's League form suffered after their European exit and they gradually slipped into the lower half of the table. They only won one of their last ten fixtures and had to settle for a mediocre 17th place in the final table. David Platt was again the leading scorer, with 19 goals.

JOZEF VENGLOS

Reign: 1990-91
Honours: None
Highest League finish: 17th in 1990-91
Best F.A. Cup Run: Round 3 in 1990-91
Best League Cup Run: Quarter-final in 1990-91
Best European Run: UEFA Cup Round 2 in 1990-91

1991-1992 SEASON

The disappointing Dr Venglos was dismissed during the summer and Ron Atkinson was lured from Sheffield Wednesday to replace him. Despite an opening day victory at Atkinson's former club, Villa got off to a mixed start, winning only three of their first 11 games and were tipped out of the League Cup (on the away goals rule) by Second Division Grimsby Town.

Five successive wins lifted them into the top four, before their challenge wilted in the winter when they scored just once in 11 matches. A late burst of five wins from the last eight games allowed Atkinson's team to finish in a respectable seventh place. Former West Bromwich Albion and Coventry City striker Cyrille Regis (in his first season at Villa Park) and the Tobago-born Dwight Yorke were the joint top scorers (with 11 apiece). Among the men who left Villa Park in 1991-92 was Blackburn-bound Gordon Cowans who made 403 League appearances (49 goals) for the club (in two spells).

Aston Villa's hopes of lifting the F.A. Cup grew with victories at Tottenham, Derby and Swindon; but were then punctured by a single goal defeat in an Anfield quarter-final.

1992-1993 SEASON

Ron Atkinson strengthened his squad with two Liverpool players. Midfielder Ray Houghton joined during the summer of 1993, while striker Dean Saunders arrived in September, with his new side lodged in mid-division. Results gradually improved after another mixed start and then four straight wins at the start of the second half of the season moved them into second place behind Manchester United. Although the goals dried up again, Villa fought tenaciously to edge to the top of the table. However, the inaugural Premier League title was to prove elusive. The last three games ended in defeat and Villa had to be satisfied with second place, ten points behind Manchester United.

Yet again it was a lack of fire-power that proved a curse. Dean Saunders finished as the top goalscorer (with 13), while Dalian Atkinson bagged 11 out of a total of only 57. Nevertheless, to finish as the runners-up was an excellent effort with Paul McGrath, Earl Barrett and Steve Staunton ever-present and superb in defence. Another defender Shaun Teale missed three games, but was equally efficient.

The Villans exited both cups at the fourth round stage in 1992-93. Wimbledon yet again knocked them out of the F.A. Cup and Ipswich Town derailed them in the League Cup.

1993-1994 SEASON

Despite an early home defeat by Manchester United, Villa made a positive start to 1993-94 and four consecutive wins in October and November took them into second place. However, their failure to put away chances hampered them and they drifted down the table following a six match winless run. Ron Atkinson's side eventually had to settle for a 10th place finish. 10-goal Dean Saunders was the main marksman, while Dalian Atkinson netted eight times. Tony Daley made his 233rd and last League appearance (31 goals) for Villa in 1993-94.

Villa started their UEFA Cup campaign by knocking out Slovan Bratislava. In the second round, a goal by Saunders allowed them to hold La Coruna Deportivo away from home. Sadly, it was the Spanish side that netted the only goal in the second leg. There was little joy in the F.A. Cup either, with second-flight Bolton Wanderers beating them 1-0 in a fifth round tie at Burnden Park. But Aston Villa did collect one piece of silverware in 1993-94, when the League Cup was lifted for the fourth time in the club's history.

After beating Birmingham City away and at home, they pulled off excellent wins at Sunderland, Arsenal and Tottenham to earn a two-legged semi-final with second-flight Tranmere Rovers.

Rovers won the first game at Prenton Park 3-1 and after a Breathtaking 90 minutes at Villa Park the scoreline on the night read 3-1 to the Villans. Extra-time produced no further goals and a trip to Wembley Stadium ended up being decided by a penalty shoot-out. Villa showed the cooler nerves to triumph 5-4!

In the Final Aston Villa faced hot favourites Manchester United, who were to go on to do the 'Double'. However, on 27th March, Ron Atkinson out-thought his Old Trafford successor, Alex Ferguson, by employing five men in midfield. Having blocked out their opponents' supply lines, Saunders netted twice (with one from the spot) and Dalian Atkinson bagged another to give Villa a 3-1 win.

The goalscorers' team-mates on the day that the Coca-Cola Cup was lifted were: goalkeeper Mark Bosnich, Earl Barrett, Steve Staunton, Shaun Teale, Paul McGrath, Kevin Richardson, Andy Townsend, Graham Fenton, Daley and substitute Neil Cox.

1994-1995 SEASON

The previous campaign's League Cup success gave Villa another taste of UEFA Cup football in 1994-95. After defeating Internazionale, on penalties, in a dramatic first round tie at Villa Park, the Villans exited in disappointing fashion, on away goals, to Trabzonspor in the second round.

Meanwhile, Villa had been under-performing in the League. And on 10th November, after a dismal spell when his side collected only one point from nine games, it was announced that Ron Atkinson had been sacked. Villa old boy Brian Little moved from a similar position at Leicester City to become Atkinson's successor.

Villa's hold on the League Cup slipped when they lost 4-1 at Crystal Palace in the fourth round. There was also a fourth round exit in the F.A. Cup, at Maine Road. Little's side also struggled in the League and only managed to secure safety on the final day of the campaign. They drew 1-1 at Norwich to finish 18th, just one place and three points above the relegation line. 15-goal Dean Saunders was the club's leading scorer in 1994-95.

RON ATKINSON

Reign: 1991-94
Honours: League Cup
Highest League finish: 2nd in 1992-93
Best F.A. Cup Run: Quarter-final in 1991-92
Best League Cup Run: Winners in 1993-94
Best European Run: UEFA Cup Round 2 in 1993-94 and 1994-95

1995-1996 SEASON

Brian Little's first full season at the helm exceeded the expectations of most pundits. His side finished fourth in the Premiership and also embarked on two lengthy cup runs. And, for the second time in three seasons, it was necessary to reshuffle the contents of the Villa Park trophy cabinet.

In the F.A. Cup, Little's team side-stepped Gravesend & Northfleet, Sheffield United, Ipswich Town and Nottingham Forest en route to a semi-final meeting with Liverpool. Unfortunately, the Reds proved too strong for them at Old Trafford.

Aston Villa went all the way in the League Cup. Peterborough United, Stockport County, Queen's Park Rangers and Wolves were defeated en route to two semi-final meetings with Arsenal. Villa had a slight psychological advantage after the first leg at Highbury ended all-square, with Dwight Yorke bagging both goals for the visitors. A crowd of 39,334 witnessed a goalless second leg allowing Villa to progress to Wembley on the away goals rule.

Leeds United formed the opposition at Wembley. Little's side took control of the match early on, with Howard Wilkinson's cautious tactics playing straight into Villa's hands. Savo Milosevic, Ian Taylor and Yorke all got on the scoresheet as Leeds capitulated by a 3-0 scoreline.

In addition to the three scorers, the players that ensured that Aston Villa lifted the Coca-Cola Cup again on 24th March 1996 were: Mark Bosnich, Gary Charles, Alan Wright, Gareth Southgate, Paul McGrath, Ugo Ehiogu, Mark Draper and Andy Townsend.

Villa were very consistent in the League during the 1995-96 campaign. Their lowest position in the table was seventh and for a short spell early on they sat in second place. They eventually finished in fourth, 19 points behind the champions Manchester United. Yorke was the club's top goalscorer (with 17), while the erratic Milosevic contributed 12 League goals. Nigel Spink made his 361st and last League appearance for Villa in 1995-96.

1996-1997 SEASON

Aston Villa were one of the most respected teams in the Premiership in 1996-97 and but for three 'sleepy' spells at various stages would have finished a lot nearer the champions (Manchester United) than the fifth place that they had to be content with at the season's close. Brian Little's side never quite managed to climb into the top three, but only briefly slipped as low as ninth place.

It was a fairly injury-free campaign with ten outfielders starting more than 20 of the 38 games, while the keeper's jersey was shared by Michael Oakes and Mark Bosnich. Dwight Yorke was the leading scorer (with another 17-goal haul), while Savo Milosevic netted nine times.

The Villans stumbled at the fourth round stage of both domestic cup competitions. Wimbledon knocked them out of the League Cup, while Derby County ejected them from the F.A. Cup at the Baseball Ground.

Villa's UEFA Cup adventure in 1996-97 lasted only two games. A late goal gave Helsingborg a 1-1 draw at Villa Park and a goalless second leg saw the Swedes progress.

1997-1998 SEASON

Villa made a shocking start with four successive defeats to lie rock bottom of the early League table. They responded with three straight wins to climb into the top half of the table. However, they gradually slipped backwards, winning only five of their next 20 fixtures.

West Ham United and Coventry City proved too strong in the League Cup and F.A. Cup, respectively, but Aston Villa still had hopes of winning the UEFA Cup when Brian Little resigned on 24th February. The board reacted quickly to recruit one of their old players and former assistant-manager John Gregory. His arrival from Wycombe Wanderers immediately brought a fresh zest into Villa's play. They immediately secured a 2-0 home win over Liverpool, with a highly delighted Stan Collymore bagging both goals against his old team-mates.

In fact Villa won nine out of their last 11 League fixtures to climb eight places up to seventh place. Their final position was their highest of the campaign. Dwight Yorke was again the leading scorer (with 12), four more than Julian Joachim.

The UEFA Cup run began with two tight matches with Bordeaux. The only goal was scored by Savo Milosevic in the second period of extra-time of the return leg at Villa Park. Another determined display ensured another goalless match at Athletic Bilbao and Villa progressed by winning the home leg 2-1.

The quarter-final clashes with Atletico Madrid came four months later, with Gregory having taken his place at the helm. The first game in Spain went the way of the home side courtesy of a first half penalty. The Spaniards also netted during the first half at Villa Park and, in spite of goals by Ian Taylor and Collymore, at the end of the game the bulk of the 39,163 crowd dispersed disappointed as the club dropped out on the away goals rule.

BRIAN LITTLE

Reign: 1994-98
Honours: League Cup
Highest League finish: 4th in 1996-97
Best F.A. Cup Run: Semi-final in 1995-96
Best League Cup Run: Winners in 1995-96
Best European Run: UEFA Cup Quarter-final in 1997-98

1998-1999 SEASON

Aston Villa made a wonderful start to the campaign and did not lose until their 13th League fixture. They registered eight wins in the process to sit proudly at the top of the Premiership table. Dwight Yorke played little part in this run, having joined Manchester United for a club record fee of £12.6 million, after wearing claret and blue just once in 1998-99. All-told he made 231 League appearances (73 goals) for the Villans.

Villa slipped off the top of the table after losing (for the third time) at Blackburn on Boxing Day. They briefly headed the table again but all hopes of winning the title evaporated with a ten match winless run that yielded just three points. John Gregory's side eventually had to settle for sixth place, 24 points adrift of Manchester United. Julian Joachim was the principal scorer (with 14), while Dion Dublin contributed 11 goals.

Villa crashed out of the League Cup 4-1 at Chelsea, in the third round, while there was only marginally more joy in the F.A. Cup, before Second Division Fulham scalped them 2-0 at Villa Park, in the fourth round.

There was more Spanish despair in the UEFA Cup, with Gregory's team meeting Celta Vigo after seeing off Stromgodset in the first round. A 1-0 win in Spain suggested that Villa would reach the latter stages again. However, Celta Vigo were even stronger opponents in the second leg and Villa were spun out 3-1 on the night and 3-2 on aggregate.

1999-2000 SEASON

Aston Villa won four of their first six fixtures of 1999-2000 to lie second in the early tables. Unfortunately, they lost their way and, after a nine match winless run, slipped to 15th place. However, only two of the last 20 games ended in defeat and John Gregory's side finished in a very respectable sixth place. Dion Dublin was the top scorer (with 12 goals), while Julian Joachim contributed six goals.

The Villans also embarked on two excellent cup runs in 1999-2000. They side-stepped Chester City, Manchester United and Southampton en route to a quarter-final clash with West Ham United at the Boleyn Ground.

The Hammers enjoyed victory in a penalty shoot-out after the tie finished all square after extra-time. However, West Ham had brought on Manny Omoyinmi from the bench, who had earlier in the season appeared in the competition for Gillingham (while on loan). Consequently, the tie was ordered to be replayed, again in East London. This time the Villans came from behind to win 3-1 after extra-time. Sadly, Gregory's men ran out of luck in the two-legged semi-final. It was Leicester City who scored the only goal during the 180 minutes and the Villa faithful experienced disappointment.

Villa progressed even further in the F.A. Cup, a run that gave their supporters the opportunity to visit Wembley Stadium twice during the year it closed. Darlington, Southampton, Leeds United and Everton were beaten by single goal margins to take the Villans into the last four and a meeting with Bolton Wanderers at the National Stadium.

A crowd of 62,828 witnessed a very tight semi-final that went to extra-time. Neither side could tuck home a goal in open play and so the tie went to a shoot-out. Villa showed the cooler nerves, winning 4-1 to earn a trip back to the Twin Towers and a meeting with Chelsea. Unfortunately, Aston Villa's first F.A. Cup Final in 43 years ended in disappointment. Gregory's men worked hard, but it was the Londoners' Roberto Di Matteo who bagged the only goal to inflict Aston Villa's third F.A. Cup final defeat.

2000-2001 SEASON

The Villans overcame a sluggish start in 2000-01 to climb into the top five. However, five straight defeats at the turn of the year knocked them back into mid-division and some improved form was required during the last two months of the campaign to enable an eighth place finish. Despite the January arrival of Juan Pablo Angel from River Plate (for a club record fee of £9.5 million), John Gregory's side were hampered by a lack of fire-power, Dion Dublin was the top scorer again, but only netted eight times – one more than Julian Joachim. Among those who left Villa Park during the campaign was Ugo Ehiogu, who joined Middlesbrough after making

237 League appearances (12 goals) in a claret and blue shirt.

Villa's League Cup run lasted just one game on their own ground, where they slipped up against Manchester City. There was also a Villa Park exit in the F.A. Cup, with this time Leicester City triumphing in the fourth round.

The Villans also participated in the Intertoto Cup in 2000-01, entering at the quarter-final stage and beating Pribram. However, any hopes of gaining a late passport into the UEFA Cup evaporated when then lost 3-1, on aggregate, to Celta Vigo.

2001-2002 SEASON

Aston Villa finished in the top eight of the Premiership for the seventh successive campaign, in 2001-02, but long before the season's end they had a change at managerial level forced upon them.

John Gregory's side only lost one of their first ten League fixtures and sat at the top of the table at the end of October. However, less than three months later, with his side still seventh in the table, Gregory handed in his resignation. He believed the team was being under-funded. Former manager Graham Taylor took over again, initially on a temporary basis and, despite a run of only one win in 13 games, Villa finished in eighth spot again. Juan Pablo Angel and Darius Vassell were the joint leading goalscorers (with 12 apiece).

There was little joy in the cup competitions during the 2001-02 campaign, with early exits at Villa Park to second-flight Sheffield Wednesday (in the League Cup) and Manchester United (in the F.A. Cup).

Success in the Intertoto Cup gave Villa another opportunity in the UEFA Cup. Gregory's side knocked out Slaven Belupo, Rennes and, in the Final, Basle to be one of the three winners of the Intertoto Cup (along with Troyes and Paris St Germain). Involvement in the UEFA Cup was less glorious, though, with Varteks sliding them out of the competition on the away goals rule.

JOHN GREGORY

Reign: 1998-2002
Highest League finish: 6th in 1998-99 and 1999-2000
Best F.A. Cup Run: Final in 1999-2000
Best League Cup Run: Semi-final in 1999-2000
Best European Run: UEFA Cup Quarter-final in 1997-98 – John Gregory became manager after Round 3 and oversaw the quarter-final defeat.

2002-2003 SEASON

For the third successive season, Aston Villa warmed up for the Premiership campaign by entering the Intertoto Cup. This time there was to be no glory, despite a quarter-final triumph over FC Zurich. Graham Taylor's team then found Lille too tough for them and went down 3-1 on aggregate.

Villa's League programme opened with four defeats from the first six matches and Taylor's side never really recovered to make any lasting impact on the top half of the table. After only two of the last 12 games ended in victory they had to settle for 16th place, just three points and two places above relegated West Ham United. Dion Dublin top scored (with 10 goals), while Vassell was on the scoresheet eight times.

Alan Wright made his 260th and last League appearance (5 goals) for Villa in 2002-03, while Steve Staunton's second spell at the club also came to and end. The Republic of Ireland defender made 281 League appearances (16 goals) and won a club record 64 caps while on Villa's books. Another man to represent Villa for the last time in 2002-03 was Ian Taylor, who made 233 League appearances (28 goals).

Taylor's side reached the quarter-final of the League Cup, defeating Luton Town, Oxford United and Preston North End before crashing out 4-3 at home to Liverpool. A even bigger defeat at Villa Park followed, in the F.A. Cup, when Blackburn Rovers triumphed 4-1.

GRAHAM TAYLOR

Reign: 1987-1990 and 2002-03
Highest League finish: 2nd in 1989-90
Best F.A. Cup Run: Quarter-final in 1989-90
Best League Cup Run: Quarter-final in 1988-89 and 2002-03
Best European Run: Intertoto Cup Semi-final in 2002-03

2003-2004 SEASON

The former Leeds United manager David O'Leary was appointed manager during the summer of 2003. Villa made a very sluggish start to the campaign and found themselves in the relegation zone, after winning just two of their first 13 League fixtures. They were still in the bottom three in mid-December before O'Leary galvanised them and they gradually climbed the table.

Villa had a fantastic second half of the season and, with two matches remaining, had a chance of qualifying for the Champions League. After extending their unbeaten run to eight games by drawing at Southampton, defeat against Manchester United, at Villa Park, consigned them to sixth place. The Villans finished five points short of a Champions League place and were edged out of an UEFA Cup spot on goal difference (by Newcastle United). Nevertheless, it was still a great achievement by O'Leary, who appeared to get the best out of the likes of Gareth Barry, Jlloyd Samuel and 16-goal Juan Pablo Angel. The Colombian was the club's leading scorer, while Darius Vassell bagged nine goals to cement his place in the full England squad. Thomas Sorensen had an excellent season between the posts (after moving from Sunderland), while Nolberto Solano quickly became a fans' favourite after his mid-season transfer from Newcastle. Among the men to represent Villa for the last time in 2003-02 was Dion Dublin (who netted 48 goals in 155 League games).

O'Leary's side reached the last four of the League Cup by knocking out Wycombe Wanderers, Leicester City, Crystal Palace and Chelsea. The semi-final first leg, at Bolton, ended in a disappointing 5-2 defeat. Villa Park goals by Thomas Hitzlsperger and Samuel were not quite enough to prevent the Trotters clinching a place in the final, 5-4 on aggregate. Manchester United came from behind to knock Villa out of the F.A. Cup in a third round tie at Villa Park.

Despite narrowly missing out on qualifying for Europe, the mood around Villa Park was extremely positive in the summer of 2004. With the likes of Liam Ridgewell, Peter Whittingham and the Moore brothers (Stefan and Luke) forcing open the first-team door, David O'Leary has an abundance of young talent at his disposal.

DAVID O'LEARY

Reign: From 2003
Honours: None
Highest League finish: 6th in 2003-04
Best F.A. Cup Run: Round 3 in 2003-04
Best League Cup Run: Semi-final in 2003-04

Villa Park as it looked during the late 1980s before recommendations of the
Taylor Report led to all-seater Stadia.

The redevelopment of the ground after the Taylor Report means that Villa Park is still regarded as one of the best stadia in England.

The famous Holte End, pictured below, holds 13,500 fans on matchdays.

Season 1974/75

DIVISION TWO

Manchester United	42	26	9	7	66	30	61
Aston Villa	**42**	**25**	**8**	**9**	**79**	**32**	**58**
Norwich City	42	20	13	9	58	37	53
Sunderland	42	19	13	10	65	35	51
Bristol City	42	21	8	13	47	33	50
West Bromwich Albion	42	18	9	15	54	42	45
Blackpool	42	14	17	11	38	33	45
Hull City	42	15	14	13	40	53	44
Fulham	42	13	16	13	44	39	42
Bolton Wanderers	42	15	12	15	45	41	42
Oxford United	42	15	12	15	41	51	42
Orient	42	11	20	11	28	39	42
Southampton	42	15	11	16	53	54	41
Notts County	42	12	16	14	49	59	40
York City	42	14	10	18	51	55	38
Nottingham Forest	42	12	14	16	43	55	38
Portsmouth	42	12	13	17	44	54	37
Oldham Athletic	42	10	15	17	40	48	35
Bristol Rovers	42	12	11	19	42	64	35
Millwall	42	10	12	20	44	56	32
Cardiff City	42	9	14	19	36	62	32
Sheffield Wednesday	42	5	11	26	29	64	21

Season 1975/76

DIVISION ONE

Liverpool	42	23	14	5	66	31	60
Queen's Park Rangers	42	24	11	7	67	33	59
Manchester United	42	23	10	9	68	42	56
Derby County	42	21	11	10	75	58	53
Leeds United	42	21	9	12	65	46	51
Ipswich Town	42	16	14	12	54	48	46
Leicester City	42	13	19	10	48	51	45
Manchester City	42	16	11	15	64	46	43
Tottenham Hotspur	42	14	15	13	63	63	43
Norwich City	42	16	10	16	58	58	42
Everton	42	15	12	15	60	66	42
Stoke City	42	15	11	16	48	50	41
Middlesbrough	42	15	10	17	46	45	40
Coventry City	42	13	14	15	47	57	40
Newcastle United	42	15	9	18	71	62	39
Aston Villa	**42**	**11**	**17**	**14**	**51**	**59**	**39**
Arsenal	42	13	10	19	47	53	36
West Ham United	42	13	10	19	48	71	36
Birmingham City	42	13	7	22	57	75	33
Wolverhampton Wanderers	42	10	10	22	51	68	30
Burnley	42	9	10	23	43	66	28
Sheffield United	42	6	10	26	33	82	22

Season 1976/77

DIVISION ONE

Liverpool	42	23	11	8	62	33	57
Manchester City	42	21	14	7	60	34	56
Ipswich Town	42	22	8	12	66	39	52
Aston Villa	**42**	**22**	**7**	**13**	**76**	**50**	**51**
Newcastle United	42	18	13	11	64	49	49
Manchester United	42	18	11	13	71	62	47
West Bromwich Albion	42	16	13	13	62	56	45
Arsenal	42	16	11	15	64	59	43
Everton	42	14	14	14	62	64	42
Leeds United	42	15	12	15	48	51	42
Leicester City	42	12	18	12	47	60	42
Middlesbrough	42	14	13	15	40	45	41
Birmingham City	42	13	12	17	63	61	38
Queen's Park Rangers	42	13	12	17	47	52	38
Derby County	42	9	19	14	50	55	37
Norwich City	42	14	9	19	47	64	37
West Ham United	42	11	14	17	46	65	36
Bristol City	42	11	13	18	38	48	35
Coventry City	42	10	15	17	48	59	35
Sunderland	42	11	12	19	46	54	34
Stoke City	42	10	14	18	28	51	34
Tottenham Hotspur	42	12	9	21	48	72	33

Season 1977/78

DIVISION ONE

Nottingham Forest	42	25	14	3	69	24	64
Liverpool	42	24	9	9	65	34	57
Everton	42	22	11	9	76	45	55
Manchester City	42	20	12	10	74	51	52
Arsenal	42	21	10	11	60	37	52
West Bromwich Albion	42	18	14	10	62	53	50
Coventry City	42	18	12	12	75	62	48
Aston Villa	**42**	**18**	**10**	**14**	**57**	**42**	**46**
Leeds United	42	18	10	14	63	53	46
Manchester United	42	16	10	16	67	63	42
Birmingham City	42	16	9	17	55	60	41
Derby County	42	14	13	15	54	59	41
Norwich City	42	11	18	13	52	66	40
Middlesbrough	42	12	15	15	42	54	39
Wolverhampton Wands.	42	12	12	18	51	64	36
Chelsea	42	11	14	17	46	69	36
Bristol City	42	11	13	18	49	53	35
Ipswich Town	42	11	13	18	47	61	35
Queen's Park Rangers	42	9	15	18	47	64	33
West Ham United	42	12	8	22	52	69	32
Newcastle United	42	6	10	26	42	78	22
Leicester City	42	5	12	25	26	70	22

Season 1978/79

DIVISION ONE

Liverpool	42	30	8	4	85	16	68
Nottingham Forest	42	21	18	3	61	26	60
West Bromwich Albion	42	24	11	7	72	35	59
Everton	42	17	17	8	52	40	51
Leeds United	42	18	14	10	70	52	50
Ipswich Town	42	20	9	13	63	49	49
Arsenal	42	17	14	11	61	48	48
Aston Villa	**42**	**15**	**16**	**11**	**59**	**49**	**46**
Manchester United	42	15	15	12	60	63	45
Coventry City	42	14	16	12	58	68	44
Tottenham Hotspur	42	13	15	14	48	61	41
Middlesbrough	42	15	10	17	57	50	40
Bristol City	42	15	10	17	47	51	40
Southampton	42	12	16	14	47	53	40
Manchester City	42	13	13	16	58	56	39
Norwich City	42	7	23	12	51	57	37
Bolton Wanderers	42	12	11	19	54	75	35
Wolverhampton Wands.	42	13	8	21	44	68	34
Derby County	42	10	11	21	44	71	31
Queen's Park Rangers	42	6	13	23	45	73	25
Birmingham City	42	6	10	26	37	64	22
Chelsea	42	5	10	27	44	92	20

Season 1979/80

DIVISION ONE

Liverpool	42	25	10	7	81	30	60
Manchester United	42	24	10	8	65	35	58
Ispwich	42	22	9	11	68	39	53
Arsenal	42	18	16	8	52	36	52
Nottingham Forest	42	20	8	14	63	43	48
Wolverhampton Wands.	42	19	9	14	58	47	47
Aston Villa	**42**	**16**	**14**	**12**	**51**	**50**	**46**
Southampton	42	18	9	15	65	53	45
Middlesbrough	42	16	12	14	50	44	44
West Bromwich Albion	42	11	19	12	54	50	41
Leeds United	42	13	14	15	46	50	40
Norwich City	42	13	14	15	58	66	40
Crystal Palace	42	12	16	14	41	50	40
Tottenham Hotspur	42	15	10	17	52	62	40
Coventry City	42	16	7	19	56	66	39
Brighton & Hove Albion	42	11	15	16	47	57	37
Manchester City	42	12	13	17	43	66	37
Stoke City	42	13	10	19	44	58	36
Everton	42	9	17	16	43	51	35
Bristol City	42	9	13	20	37	66	31
Derby County	42	11	8	23	47	67	30
Bolton Wanderers	42	5	15	22	38	73	25

Season 1980/81

DIVISION ONE

Aston Villa	42	26	8	8	72	40	60
Ipswich Town	42	23	10	9	77	43	56
Arsenal	42	19	15	8	61	45	53
West Bromwich Albion	42	20	12	10	60	42	52
Liverpool	42	17	17	8	62	42	51
Southampton	42	20	10	12	76	56	50
Nottingham Forest	42	19	12	11	62	44	50
Manchester United	42	15	18	9	51	36	48
Leeds United	42	17	10	15	39	47	44
Tottenham Hotspur	42	14	15	13	70	68	43
Stoke City	42	12	18	12	51	60	42
Manchester City	42	14	11	17	56	59	39
Birmingham City	42	13	12	17	50	61	38
Middlesbrough	42	16	5	21	53	61	37
Everton	42	13	10	19	55	58	36
Coventry City	42	13	10	19	48	68	36
Sunderland	42	14	7	21	52	53	35
Wolverhampton Wands.	42	13	9	20	43	55	35
Brighton & Hove Albion	42	14	7	21	54	67	35
Norwich City	42	13	7	22	49	73	33
Leicester City	42	13	6	23	40	67	32
Crystal Palace	42	6	7	29	47	83	19

Season 1981/82

DIVISION ONE

Liverpool	42	26	9	7	80	32	87
Ipswich Town	42	26	5	11	75	53	83
Manchester United	42	22	12	8	59	29	78
Tottenham Hotspur	42	20	11	11	67	48	71
Arsenal	42	20	11	11	48	37	71
Swansea City	42	21	6	15	58	51	69
Southampton	42	19	9	14	72	67	66
Everton	42	17	13	12	56	50	64
West Ham United	42	14	16	12	66	57	58
Manchester City	42	15	13	14	49	50	58
Aston Villa	42	15	12	15	55	53	57
Nottingham Forest	42	15	12	15	42	48	57
Brighton & Hove Albion	42	13	13	16	43	52	52
Coventry City	42	13	11	18	56	62	50
Notts County	42	13	8	21	61	69	47
Birmingham City	42	10	14	18	53	61	44
West Bromwich Albion	42	11	11	20	46	57	44
Stoke City	42	12	8	22	44	63	44
Sunderland	42	11	11	20	38	58	44
Leeds United	42	10	12	20	39	61	42
Wolverhampton Wands.	42	10	10	22	32	63	40
Middlesbrough	42	8	15	19	34	52	39

Season 1982/83

DIVISION ONE

Liverpool	42	24	10	8	87	37	82
Watford	42	22	5	15	74	57	71
Manchester United	42	19	13	10	56	38	70
Tottenham Hotspur	42	20	9	13	65	50	69
Nottingham Forest	42	20	9	13	62	50	69
Aston Villa	42	21	5	16	62	50	68
Everton	42	18	10	14	66	48	64
West Ham United	42	20	4	18	68	62	64
Ipswich Town	42	15	13	14	64	50	58
Arsenal	42	16	10	16	58	56	58
West Bromwich Albion	42	15	12	15	51	49	57
Southampton	42	15	12	15	54	58	57
Stoke City	42	16	9	17	53	64	57
Norwich City	42	14	12	16	52	58	54
Notts County	42	15	7	20	55	71	52
Sunderland	42	12	14	16	48	61	50
Birmingham City	42	12	14	16	40	55	50
Luton Town	42	12	13	17	65	84	49
Coventry City	42	13	9	20	48	59	48
Manchester City	42	13	8	21	47	70	47
Swansea City	42	10	11	21	51	69	41
Brighton & Hove Albion	42	9	13	20	38	68	40

Season 1983/84

DIVISION ONE

Liverpool	42	22	14	6	73	32	80
Southampton	42	22	11	9	66	38	77
Nottingham Forest	42	22	8	12	76	45	74
Manchester United	42	20	14	8	71	41	74
Queen's Park Rangers	42	22	7	13	67	37	73
Arsenal	42	18	9	15	74	60	63
Everton	42	16	14	12	44	42	62
Tottenham Hotspur	42	17	10	15	64	65	61
West Ham United	42	17	9	16	60	55	60
Aston Villa	42	17	9	16	59	61	60
Watford	42	16	9	17	68	77	57
Ipswich Town	42	15	8	19	55	57	53
Sunderland	42	13	13	16	42	53	52
Norwich City	42	12	15	15	48	49	51
Leicester City	42	13	12	17	65	68	51
Luton Town	42	14	9	19	53	66	51
West Bromwich Albion	42	14	9	19	48	62	51
Stoke City	42	13	11	18	44	63	50
Coventry City	42	13	11	18	57	77	50
Birmingham City	42	12	12	18	39	50	48
Notts County	42	10	11	21	50	72	41
Wolverhampton Wands.	42	6	11	25	27	80	29

Season 1984/85

DIVISION ONE

Everton	42	28	6	8	88	43	90
Liverpool	42	22	11	9	68	35	77
Tottenham Hotspur	42	23	8	11	78	51	77
Manchester United	42	22	10	10	77	47	76
Southampton	42	19	11	12	56	47	68
Chelsea	42	18	12	12	63	48	66
Arsenal	42	19	9	14	61	49	66
Sheffield Wednesday	42	17	14	11	58	45	65
Nottingham Forest	42	19	7	16	56	48	64
Aston Villa	42	15	11	16	60	60	56
Watford	42	14	13	15	81	71	55
West Bromwich Albion	42	16	7	19	58	62	55
Luton Town	42	15	9	18	57	61	54
Newcastle United	42	13	13	16	55	70	52
Leicester City	42	15	6	21	65	73	51
West Ham United	42	13	12	17	51	68	51
Ipswich Town	42	13	11	18	46	57	50
Coventry City	42	15	5	22	47	64	50
Queen's Park Rangers	42	13	11	18	53	72	50
Norwich City	42	13	10	19	46	64	49
Sunderland	42	10	10	22	40	62	40
Stoke City	42	3	8	31	24	91	17

Season 1985/86

DIVISION ONE

Liverpool	42	26	10	6	89	37	88
Everton	42	26	8	8	87	41	86
West Ham United	42	26	6	10	74	40	84
Manchester United	42	22	10	10	70	36	76
Sheffield Wednesday	42	21	10	11	63	54	73
Chelsea	42	20	11	11	57	56	71
Arsenal	42	20	9	13	49	47	69
Nottingham Forest	42	19	11	12	69	53	68
Luton Town	42	18	12	12	61	44	66
Tottenham Hotspur	42	19	8	15	74	52	65
Newcastle United	42	17	12	13	67	72	63
Watford	42	16	11	15	69	62	59
Queen's Park Rangers	42	15	7	20	53	64	52
Southampton	42	12	10	20	51	62	46
Manchester City	42	11	12	19	43	57	45
Aston Villa	42	10	14	18	51	67	44
Coventry City	42	11	10	21	48	71	43
Oxford United	42	10	12	20	62	80	42
Leicester City	42	10	12	20	54	76	42
Ipswich Town	42	11	8	23	32	55	41
Birmingham City	42	8	5	29	30	73	29
West Bromwich Albion	42	4	12	26	35	89	24

Season 1986/87

DIVISION ONE

Everton	42	26	8	8	76	31	86
Liverpool	42	23	8	11	72	42	77
Tottenham Hotspur	42	21	8	13	68	43	71
Arsenal	42	20	10	12	58	35	70
Norwich City	42	17	17	8	53	51	68
Wimbledon	42	19	9	14	57	50	66
Luton Town	42	18	12	12	47	45	66
Nottingham Forest	42	18	11	13	64	51	65
Watford	42	18	9	15	67	54	63
Coventry City	42	17	12	13	50	45	63
Manchester United	42	14	14	14	52	45	56
Southampton	42	14	10	18	69	68	52
Sheffield Wednesday	42	13	13	16	58	59	52
Chelsea	42	13	13	16	53	64	52
West Ham United	42	14	10	18	52	67	52
Queen's Park Rangers	42	13	11	18	48	64	50
Newcastle United	42	12	11	19	47	65	47
Oxford United	42	11	13	18	44	69	46
Charlton Athletic	42	11	11	20	45	55	44
Leicester City	42	11	9	22	54	76	42
Manchester City	42	8	15	19	36	57	39
Aston Villa	**42**	**8**	**12**	**22**	**45**	**79**	**36**

Season 1987/88

DIVISION TWO

Millwall	44	25	7	12	72	52	82
Aston Villa	**44**	**22**	**12**	**10**	**68**	**41**	**78**
Middlesbrough	44	22	12	10	63	36	78
Bradford City	44	22	11	11	74	54	77
Blackburn Rovers	44	21	14	9	68	52	77
Crystal Palace	44	22	9	13	86	59	75
Leeds United	44	19	12	13	61	51	69
Ipswich Town	44	19	9	16	61	52	66
Manchester City	44	19	8	17	80	60	65
Oldham Athletic	44	18	11	15	72	64	65
Stoke City	44	17	11	16	50	57	62
Swindon Town	44	16	11	17	73	60	59
Leicester City	44	16	11	17	62	61	59
Barnsley	44	15	12	17	61	62	57
Hull City	44	14	15	15	54	60	57
Plymouth Argyle	44	16	8	20	65	67	56
Bournemouth	44	13	10	21	56	68	49
Shrewsbury Town	44	11	16	17	42	54	49
Birmingham City	44	11	15	18	41	66	48
West Bromwich Albion	44	12	11	21	50	69	47
Sheffield United	44	13	7	24	45	74	46
Reading	44	10	12	22	44	70	42
Huddersfield Town	44	6	10	28	41	100	28

Season 1988/89

DIVISION ONE

Arsenal	38	22	10	6	73	36	76
Liverpool	38	22	10	6	65	28	76
Nottingham Forest	38	17	13	8	64	43	64
Norwich City	38	17	11	10	48	45	62
Derby County	38	17	7	14	40	38	58
Tottenham Hotspur	38	15	12	11	60	46	57
Coventry City	38	14	13	11	47	42	55
Everton	38	14	12	12	50	45	54
Queen's Park Rangers	38	14	11	13	43	37	53
Millwall	38	14	11	13	47	52	53
Manchester United	38	13	12	13	45	35	51
Wimbledon	38	14	9	15	50	46	51
Southampton	38	10	15	13	52	66	45
Charlton Athletic	38	10	12	16	44	58	42
Sheffield Wednesday	38	10	12	16	34	51	42
Luton Town	38	10	11	17	42	52	41
Aston Villa	**38**	**9**	**13**	**16**	**45**	**56**	**40**
Middlesbrough	38	9	12	17	44	61	39
West Ham United	38	10	8	20	37	62	38
Newcastle United	38	7	10	21	32	63	31

Season 1989/90

DIVISION ONE

Liverpool	38	23	10	5	78	37	79
Aston Villa	**38**	**21**	**7**	**10**	**57**	**38**	**70**
Tottenham Hotspur	38	19	6	13	59	47	63
Arsenal	38	18	8	12	54	38	62
Chelsea	38	16	12	10	58	50	60
Everton	38	17	8	13	57	46	59
Southampton	38	15	10	13	71	63	55
Wimbledon	38	13	16	9	47	40	55
Nottingham Forest	38	15	9	14	55	47	54
Norwich City	38	13	14	11	44	42	53
Queen's Park Rangers	38	13	11	14	45	44	50
Coventry City	38	14	7	17	39	59	49
Manchester United	38	13	9	16	46	47	48
Manchester City	38	12	12	14	43	52	48
Crystal Palace	38	13	9	16	42	66	48
Derby County	38	13	7	18	43	40	46
Luton Town	38	10	13	15	43	57	43
Sheffield Wednesday	38	11	10	17	35	51	43
Charlton Athletic	38	7	9	22	31	57	30
Millwall	38	5	11	22	39	65	26

Season 1990/91

DIVISION ONE

Arsenal	38	24	13	1	74	18	83
Liverpool	38	23	7	8	77	40	76
Crystal Palace	38	20	9	9	50	41	69
Leeds United	38	19	7	12	65	47	64
Manchester City	38	17	11	10	64	53	62
Manchester United	38	16	12	10	58	45	60
Wimbledon	38	14	14	10	53	46	56
Nottingham Forest	38	14	12	12	65	50	54
Everton	38	13	12	13	50	46	51
Tottenham Hotspur	38	11	16	11	51	50	49
Chelsea	38	13	10	15	58	69	49
Queen's Park Rangers	38	12	10	16	44	53	46
Sheffield United	38	13	7	18	36	55	46
Southampton	38	12	9	17	58	69	45
Norwich City	38	13	6	19	41	64	45
Coventry City	38	11	11	16	42	49	44
Aston Villa	**38**	**9**	**14**	**15**	**46**	**58**	**41**
Luton Town	38	10	7	21	42	61	37
Sunderland	38	8	10	20	38	60	34
Derby County	38	5	9	24	37	75	24

Arsenal had 2 points deducted
Manchester United had 1 point deducted

Season 1991/92

DIVISION ONE

Leeds United	42	22	16	4	74	37	82
Manchester United	42	21	15	6	63	33	78
Sheffield Wednesday	42	21	12	9	62	49	75
Arsenal	42	19	15	8	81	46	72
Manchester City	42	20	10	12	61	48	70
Liverpool	42	16	16	10	47	40	64
Aston Villa	**42**	**17**	**9**	**16**	**48**	**44**	**60**
Nottingham Forest	42	16	11	15	60	58	59
Sheffield United	42	16	9	17	65	63	57
Crystal Palace	42	14	15	13	53	61	57
Queen's Park Rangers	42	12	18	12	48	47	54
Everton	42	13	14	15	52	51	53
Wimbledon	42	13	14	15	53	53	53
Chelsea	42	13	14	15	50	60	53
Tottenham Hotspur	42	15	7	20	58	63	52
Southampton	42	14	10	18	39	55	52
Oldham Athletic	42	14	9	19	63	67	51
Norwich City	42	11	12	19	47	63	45
Coventry City	42	11	11	20	35	44	44
Luton Town	42	10	12	20	38	71	42
Notts County	42	10	10	22	40	62	40
West Ham United	42	9	11	22	37	59	38

Season 1992/93

F.A. PREMIER LEAGUE

Team	P	W	D	L	F	A	Pts
Manchester United	42	24	12	6	67	31	84
Aston Villa	**42**	**21**	**11**	**10**	**57**	**40**	**74**
Norwich City	42	21	9	12	61	65	72
Blackburn Rovers	42	20	11	11	68	46	71
Queen's Park Rangers	42	17	12	13	63	55	63
Liverpool	42	16	11	15	62	55	59
Sheffield Wednesday	42	15	14	13	55	51	59
Tottenham Hotspur	42	16	11	15	60	66	59
Manchester City	42	15	12	15	56	51	57
Arsenal	42	15	11	16	40	38	56
Chelsea	42	14	14	14	51	54	56
Wimbledon	42	14	12	16	56	55	54
Everton	42	15	8	19	53	55	53
Sheffield United	42	14	10	18	54	53	52
Coventry City	42	13	13	16	52	57	52
Ipswich Town	42	12	16	14	50	55	52
Leeds United	42	12	15	15	57	62	51
Southampton	42	13	11	18	54	61	50
Oldham Athletic	42	13	10	19	63	74	49
Crystal Palace	42	11	16	15	48	61	49
Middlesbrough	42	11	11	20	54	75	44
Nottingham Forest	42	10	10	22	41	62	40

Season 1993/94

F.A.PREMIERSHIP

Team	P	W	D	L	F	A	Pts
Manchester United	42	27	11	4	80	38	92
Blackburn Rovers	42	25	9	8	63	36	84
Newcastle United	42	23	8	11	82	41	77
Arsenal	42	18	17	7	53	28	71
Leeds United	42	18	16	8	65	39	70
Wimbledon	42	18	11	13	56	53	65
Sheffield Wednesday	42	16	16	10	76	54	64
Liverpool	42	17	9	16	59	55	60
Queen's Park Rangers	42	16	12	14	62	61	60
Aston Villa	**42**	**15**	**12**	**15**	**46**	**50**	**57**
Coventry City	42	14	14	14	43	45	56
Norwich City	42	12	17	13	65	61	53
West Ham United	42	13	13	16	47	58	52
Chelsea	42	13	12	17	49	53	51
Tottenham Hotspur	42	11	12	19	54	59	45
Manchester City	42	9	18	15	38	49	45
Everton	42	12	8	22	42	63	44
Southampton	42	12	7	23	49	66	43
Ipswich Town	42	9	16	17	35	58	43
Sheffield United	42	8	18	16	42	60	42
Oldham Athletic	42	9	13	20	42	68	40
Swindon Town	42	5	15	22	47	100	30

Season 1994/95

F.A. PREMIERSHIP

Team	P	W	D	L	F	A	Pts
Blackburn Rovers	42	27	8	7	80	39	89
Manchester United	42	26	10	6	77	28	88
Nottingham Forest	42	22	11	9	72	43	77
Liverpool	42	21	11	10	65	37	74
Leeds United	42	20	13	9	59	38	73
Newcastle United	42	20	12	10	67	47	72
Tottenham Hotspur	42	16	14	12	66	58	62
Queen's Park Rangers	42	17	9	16	61	59	60
Wimbledon	42	15	11	16	48	65	56
Southampton	42	12	18	12	61	63	54
Chelsea	42	13	15	14	50	55	54
Arsenal	42	13	12	17	52	49	51
Sheffield Wednesday	42	13	12	17	49	57	51
West Ham United	42	13	11	18	44	48	50
Everton	42	11	17	14	44	51	50
Coventry City	42	12	14	16	44	62	50
Manchester City	42	12	13	17	53	64	49
Aston Villa	**42**	**11**	**15**	**16**	**51**	**56**	**48**
Crystal Palace	42	11	12	19	34	49	45
Norwich City	42	10	13	19	37	54	43
Leicester City	42	6	11	25	45	80	29
Ipswich Town	42	7	6	29	36	93	27

Season 1995/96

F.A. PREMIERSHIP

Team	P	W	D	L	F	A	Pts
Manchester United	38	25	7	6	73	35	82
Newcastle United	38	24	6	8	66	37	78
Liverpool	38	20	11	7	70	34	71
Aston Villa	**38**	**18**	**9**	**11**	**52**	**35**	**63**
Arsenal	38	17	12	9	49	32	63
Everton	38	17	10	11	64	44	61
Blackburn Rovers	38	18	7	13	61	47	61
Tottenham Hotspur	38	16	13	9	50	38	61
Nottingham Forest	38	15	13	10	50	54	58
West Ham United	38	14	9	15	43	52	51
Chelsea	38	12	14	12	46	44	50
Middlesbrough	38	11	10	17	35	50	43
Leeds United	38	12	7	19	40	57	43
Wimbledon	38	10	11	17	55	70	41
Sheffield Wednesday	38	10	10	18	48	61	40
Coventry City	38	8	14	16	42	60	38
Southampton	38	9	11	18	34	52	38
Manchester City	38	9	11	18	33	58	38
Queen's Park Rangers	38	9	6	23	38	57	33
Bolton Wanderers	38	8	5	25	39	71	29

Season 1996/97

F.A. PREMIERSHIP

Team	P	W	D	L	F	A	Pts
Manchester United	38	21	12	5	76	44	75
Newcastle United	38	19	11	8	73	40	68
Arsenal	38	19	11	8	62	32	68
Liverpool	38	19	11	8	62	37	68
Aston Villa	**38**	**17**	**10**	**11**	**47**	**34**	**61**
Chelsea	38	16	11	11	58	55	59
Sheffield Wednesday	38	14	15	9	50	51	57
Wimbledon	38	15	11	12	49	46	56
Leicester City	38	12	11	15	46	54	47
Tottenham Hotspur	38	13	7	18	44	51	46
Leeds United	38	11	13	14	28	38	46
Derby County	38	11	13	14	45	58	46
Blackburn Rovers	38	9	15	14	42	43	42
West Ham United	38	10	12	16	39	48	42
Everton	38	10	12	16	44	57	42
Southampton	38	10	11	17	50	56	41
Coventry City	38	9	14	15	38	54	41
Sunderland	38	10	10	18	35	53	40
Middlesbrough	38	10	12	16	51	60	39
Nottingham Forest	38	6	16	16	31	59	34

Middlesbrough had 3 points deducted

Season 1997/98

F.A. PREMIERSHIP

Team	P	W	D	L	F	A	Pts
Arsenal	38	23	9	6	68	33	78
Manchester United	38	23	8	7	73	26	77
Liverpool	38	18	11	9	68	42	65
Chelsea	38	20	3	15	71	43	63
Leeds United	38	17	8	13	57	46	59
Blackburn Rovers	38	16	10	12	57	52	58
Aston Villa	**38**	**17**	**6**	**15**	**49**	**48**	**57**
West Ham United	38	16	8	14	56	57	56
Derby County	38	16	7	15	52	49	55
Leicester City	38	13	14	11	51	41	53
Coventry City	38	12	16	10	46	44	52
Southampton	38	14	6	18	50	55	48
Newcastle United	38	11	11	16	35	44	44
Tottenham Hotspur	38	11	11	16	44	56	44
Wimbledon	38	10	14	14	34	46	44
Sheffield Wednesday	38	12	8	18	52	67	44
Everton	38	9	13	16	41	56	40
Bolton Wanderers	38	9	13	16	41	61	40
Barnsley	38	10	5	23	37	82	35
Crystal Palace	38	8	9	21	37	71	33

Season 1998/99

F.A. PREMIERSHIP

	P	W	D	L	F	A	Pts
Manchester United	38	22	13	3	80	37	79
Arsenal	38	22	12	4	59	17	78
Chelsea	38	20	15	3	57	30	75
Leeds United	38	18	13	7	62	34	67
West Ham United	38	16	9	13	46	53	57
Aston Villa	**38**	**15**	**10**	**13**	**51**	**46**	**55**
Liverpool	38	15	9	14	68	49	54
Derby County	38	13	13	12	40	45	52
Middlesbrough	38	12	15	11	48	54	51
Leicester City	38	12	13	13	40	46	49
Tottenham Hotspur	38	11	14	13	47	50	47
Sheffield Wednesday	38	13	7	18	41	42	46
Newcastle United	38	11	13	14	48	54	46
Everton	38	11	10	17	42	47	43
Coventry City	38	11	9	18	39	51	42
Wimbledon	38	10	12	16	40	63	42
Southampton	38	11	8	19	37	64	41
Charlton Athletic	38	8	12	18	41	56	36
Blackburn Rovers	38	7	14	17	38	52	35
Nottingham Forest	38	7	9	22	35	69	30

Season 1999/2000

F.A. PREMIERSHIP

	P	W	D	L	F	A	Pts
Manchester United	38	28	7	3	97	45	91
Arsenal	38	22	7	9	73	43	73
Leeds United	38	21	6	11	58	43	69
Liverpool	38	19	10	9	51	30	67
Chelsea	38	18	11	9	53	34	65
Aston Villa	**38**	**15**	**13**	**10**	**46**	**35**	**58**
Sunderland	38	16	10	12	57	56	58
Leicester City	38	16	7	15	55	55	55
West Ham United	38	15	10	13	52	53	55
Tottenham Hotspur	38	15	8	15	57	49	53
Newcastle United	38	14	10	14	63	54	52
Middlesbrough	38	14	10	14	46	52	52
Everton	38	12	14	12	59	49	50
Coventry City	38	12	8	18	47	54	44
Southampton	38	12	8	18	45	62	44
Derby County	38	9	11	18	44	57	38
Bradford City	38	9	9	20	38	68	36
Wimbledon	38	7	12	19	46	74	33
Sheffield Wednesday	38	8	7	23	38	70	31
Watford	38	6	6	26	35	77	24

Season 2000/2001

F.A. PREMIERSHIP

	P	W	D	L	F	A	Pts
Manchester United	38	24	8	6	79	31	80
Arsenal	38	20	10	8	63	38	70
Liverpool	38	20	9	9	71	39	69
Leeds United	38	20	8	10	64	43	68
Ipswich Town	38	20	6	12	57	42	66
Chelsea	38	17	10	11	68	45	61
Sunderland	38	15	12	11	46	41	57
Aston Villa	**38**	**13**	**15**	**10**	**46**	**43**	**54**
Charlton Athletic	38	14	10	14	50	57	52
Southampton	38	14	10	14	40	48	52
Newcastle United	38	14	9	15	44	50	51
Tottenham Hotspur	38	13	10	15	47	54	49
Leicester City	38	14	6	18	39	51	48
Middlesbrough	38	9	15	14	44	44	42
West Ham United	38	10	12	16	45	50	42
Everton	38	11	9	18	45	59	42
Derby County	38	10	12	16	37	59	42
Manchester City	38	8	10	20	41	65	34
Coventry City	38	8	10	20	36	63	34
Bradford City	38	5	11	22	30	70	26

Season 2001/2002

F.A. PREMIERSHIP

	P	W	D	L	F	A	Pts
Arsenal	38	26	9	3	79	36	87
Liverpool	38	24	8	6	67	30	80
Manchester United	38	24	5	9	87	45	77
Newcastle United	38	21	8	9	74	52	71
Leeds United	38	18	12	8	53	37	66
Chelsea	38	17	13	8	66	38	64
West Ham United	38	15	8	15	48	57	53
Aston Villa	**38**	**12**	**14**	**12**	**46**	**47**	**50**
Tottenham Hotspur	38	14	8	16	49	53	50
Blackburn Rovers	38	12	10	16	55	51	46
Southampton	38	12	9	17	46	54	45
Middlesbrough	38	12	9	17	35	47	45
Fulham	38	10	14	14	36	44	44
Charlton Athletic	38	10	14	14	38	49	44
Everton	38	11	10	17	45	57	43
Bolton Wanderers	38	9	13	16	44	62	40
Sunderland	38	10	10	18	29	51	40
Ipswich Town	38	9	9	20	41	64	36
Derby County	38	8	6	24	33	63	30
Leicester City	38	5	13	20	30	64	28

Season 2002/2003

F.A. PREMIERSHIP

	P	W	D	L	F	A	Pts
Manchester United	38	25	8	5	74	34	83
Arsenal	38	23	9	6	85	42	78
Newcastle United	38	21	6	11	63	48	69
Chelsea	38	19	10	9	68	38	67
Liverpool	38	18	10	10	61	41	64
Blackburn Rovers	38	16	12	10	52	43	60
Everton	38	17	8	13	48	49	59
Southampton	38	13	13	12	43	46	52
Manchester City	38	15	6	17	47	54	51
Tottenham Hotspur	38	14	8	16	51	62	50
Middlesbrough	38	13	10	15	48	44	49
Charlton Athletic	38	14	7	17	45	56	49
Birmingham City	38	13	9	16	41	49	48
Fulham	38	13	9	16	41	50	48
Leeds United	38	14	5	19	58	57	47
Aston Villa	**38**	**12**	**9**	**17**	**42**	**47**	**45**
Bolton Wanderers	38	10	14	14	41	51	44
West Ham United	38	10	12	16	42	59	42
West Bromwich Albion	38	6	8	24	29	65	26
Sunderland	38	4	7	27	21	65	19

Season 2003/2004

F.A. PREMIERSHIP

	P	W	D	L	F	A	Pts
Arsenal	38	26	12	0	73	26	90
Chelsea	38	24	7	7	67	30	79
Manchester United	38	23	6	9	64	35	75
Liverpool	38	16	12	10	55	37	60
Newcastle United	38	13	17	8	52	40	56
Aston Villa	**38**	**15**	**11**	**12**	**48**	**44**	**56**
Charlton Athletic	38	14	11	13	51	51	53
Bolton Wanderers	38	14	11	13	48	56	53
Fulham	38	14	10	14	52	46	52
Birmingham City	38	12	14	12	43	48	50
Middlesbrough	38	13	9	16	44	52	48
Southampton	38	12	11	15	44	45	47
Portsmouth	38	12	9	17	47	54	45
Tottenham Hotspur	38	13	6	19	47	57	45
Blackburn Rovers	38	12	8	18	51	59	44
Manchester City	38	9	14	15	55	54	41
Everton	38	9	12	17	45	57	39
Leicester City	38	6	15	17	48	65	33
Leeds United	38	8	9	21	40	79	33
Wolverhampton Wanderers	38	7	12	19	38	77	33

1974-75

1	Aug	17	(a)	York C	D	1-1	Graydon	8,740
2		20	(a)	Hull C	D	1-1	Robson	8,712
3		24	(h)	Norwich C	D	1-1	Graydon	23,297
4		28	(h)	Hull C	W	6-0	Morgan 3, Graydon, Little B, Hamilton	18,973
5		31	(a)	Bolton W	L	0-1		12,976
6	Sep	7	(h)	Orient	W	3-1	Morgan, Graydon 2	16,802
7		14	(a)	Bristol R	L	0-2		14,035
8		21	(h)	Millwall	W	3-0	Graydon 3 (1 pen)	21,375
9		28	(a)	Southampton	D	0-0		18,599
10	Oct	2	(h)	Nottingham F	W	3-0	Graydon, Hamilton, Leonard	20,357
11		5	(a)	Oldham A	W	2-1	Graydon, Hicks (og)	15,574
12		12	(h)	Blackpool	W	1-0	Graydon	25,763
13		19	(a)	Sunderland	D	0-0		33,232
14		26	(h)	Sheffield W	W	3-1	Phillips, Nicholl, Graydon (pen)	23,977
15	Nov	2	(a)	Fulham	L	1-3	Little B	10,979
16		9	(h)	Notts Co	L	0-1		22,162
17		16	(a)	Manchester U	L	1-2	Hamilton	55,615
18		23	(h)	Portsmouth	W	2-0	Hamilton, Little B	16,827
19		29	(h)	Oxford U	D	0-0		18,554
20	Dec	7	(a)	Bristol C	L	0-1		13,390
21		14	(h)	York C	W	4-0	Graydon, Nicholl, Little B, Hamilton	15,840
22		21	(a)	West Brom A	L	0-2		23,011
23		26	(h)	Bristol R	W	1-0	Graydon	21,557
24		28	(a)	Cardiff C	L	1-3	Hamilton	11,040
25	Jan	11	(h)	Bristol C	W	2-0	Little B, Hamilton	21,762
26		18	(a)	Oxford U	W	2-1	Little B, Nicholl	9,872
27	Feb	1	(a)	Notts Co	W	3-1	Little B 2, Carrodus	17,275
28		8	(h)	Fulham	D	1-1	Nicholl	28,533
29		18	(a)	Portsmouth	W	3-2	Carrodus, Little B, Graydon	13,354
30		22	(h)	Manchester U	W	2-0	Graydon, Aitken	39,156
31	Mar	5	(h)	Bolton W	D	0-0		39,322
32		8	(a)	Nottingham F	W	3-2	Graydon 2, Little B	20,205
33		15	(h)	Southampton	W	3-0	Leonard, Graydon, Holmes (og)	31,967
34		22	(a)	Orient	L	0-1		9,466
35		29	(a)	West Brom A	W	3-1	Leonard 2, Hamilton	47,574
36	Apr	1	(a)	Millwall	W	3-1	Hamilton (pen), Little B, Leonard	13,115
37		9	(h)	Cardiff C	W	2-0	Little B 2	32,748
38		12	(h)	Oldham A	W	5-0	Little B 3, Hamilton, Hicks (og)	36,224
39		19	(a)	Blackpool	W	3-0	Phillips, Hatton (og), Little B	20,762
40		23	(a)	Sheffield W	W	4-0	Leonard, Little B 2, Ross (pen)	23,605
41		26	(h)	Sunderland	W	2-0	Ross (pen), Little B	57,266
42		30	(a)	Norwich C	W	4-1	Leonard, Gidman, McDonald, Carrodus	35,999

FINAL LEAGUE POSITION: 2nd in Division Two

Appearances

Sub. Appearances

Goals

Cumbes	Gidman	Aitken	Ross	Nicholl	Robson	Graydon	Little B	Morgan	Hamilton	Carrodus	Moseley	Betts	Brown	Campbell	McDonald	Hunt	Leonard	Findlay	Little A	McMahon	Phillips	Pimblett	Rioch N	Masefield	No.
1	2	3	4	5	6	7	8	9	10	11															1
1	2	3	4	5	6	7	8	9	10	11															2
1	2	3	4	5	6	7	8	9	10					11											3
	2	3	4	5	6	7	8	9	10	11								1							4
		3	4	5	2	7	8	9	10	11	1		6												5
	2	3	4	5	6	7	8	9	10		1										11				6
	2	3	4	5	6	7		9		11	1			10							8				7
1	2	3	4	5	6			9	8	11				10*							12				8
1	2	3	4	5	6	7			8	11							9				10				9
1	2	3	4	5	6	7			8	11							9				10				10
1	2	3	4	5		7				11		8					9		6		10				11
1	2	3	4	5	6	7		9	8	11											10				12
1		3	4	5	6	7		9	8	11											10		2		13
1		3	4*	5	6	7	12	9	8	11											10		2		14
1	2	3	4	5	6	7	11	9*	8				12								10				15
1		3	4	5	6	7	11		8*				12	9							10		2		16
1		3	4	5	2	7	8		10	11					6		9								17
1		3	4	5	2	7	8		10	11					6		9								18
1		3	4	5	2	7	8		10	11					6					12	9*				19
1		3	4	5	2	7	8		10	11					6				9						20
1		3	4	5	2	7	8		10	11					6		9								21
1		3	4	5	2	7	8		10*	11				12			9				6				22
1		3	4	5	2	7	8		10	11*				12			9				6				23
1		3	4	5	2	7	8		10	11*					12		9				6				24
1		3	4	5	2	7	8		10						6		9				11				25
1		3	4	5	2	7	8		10	11					6		9								26
1		3	4	5	2	7	8		10	11					6		9								27
1		3	4	5	2	7	8		10	11					6		9								28
1		3	4		2	7	8			11					6		9				10	5			29
1		3	4	5	2	7*	8			11					6		9				10		12		30
1		3	4	5	2	7	8		10	11					6		9								31
1		3	4	5	2	7	8		10	11					6		9			12					32
1		3	4	5	2	7	8		10	11					6		9								33
1		3	4	5	2	7	8		10	11					6		9								34
1		3	4	5	2	7	8		10	11							9				6				35
1		3	4	5	2	7*	8		10	11					12		9				6				36
1		3	4	5	2	7*	8		10	11					12		9				6				37
1		3	4	5	2		8		10	11					7		9				6				38
1		3	4	5	2		8		10	11					7		9				6				39
1		3	4	5	2		8		10*	11					7	12	9				6				40
1	12	3	4	5	2		8			11					7	10*	9				6				41
1	6	3	4	5	2		8		10	11					7		9					8			42
38	13	42	42	41	41	37	33	12	37	35	3	1	9	6	15	1	22	1	2	2	23	2	4		
	1	1				1					2	1	1	3	1			1			2		1		
	1	1	2	4	1	19	20	4	10	3				1			7				2				

1975-76

1	Aug	16	(h)	Leeds U	L	1-2	Phillips	46,026
2		19	(a)	QPR	D	1-1	Leonard	21,986
3		23	(a)	Norwich C	L	3-5	Graydon 2 (1 pen), Aitken	21,797
4		27	(h)	Manchester C	W	1-0	Leonard	35,212
5		30	(h)	Coventry C	W	1-0	Graydon	41,026
6	Sep	6	(a)	Newcastle U	L	0-3		34,668
7		13	(h)	Arsenal	W	2-0	Phillips, Leonard	34,474
8		20	(a)	Liverpool	L	0-3		42,779
9		23	(a)	Wolves	D	0-0		33,344
10		27	(h)	Birmingham C	W	2-1	Hamilton, Little	53,782
11	Oct	4	(a)	Middlesbrough	D	0-0		24,102
12		11	(h)	Tottenham H	D	1-1	Gray	40,048
13		18	(a)	Everton	L	1-2	Nicholl	30,376
14		25	(h)	Burnley	D	1-1	Noble (og)	34,242
15	Nov	1	(a)	Ipswich T	L	0-3		24,691
16		8	(h)	Sheffield U	W	5-1	Gray, Hamilton 2, Deehan, Graydon (pen)	30,053
17		15	(a)	Manchester U	L	0-2		51,682
18		22	(h)	Everton	W	3-1	Gray 2, McNaught (og)	33,949
19		29	(h)	Leicester C	D	1-1	Graydon	36,388
20	Dec	6	(a)	Stoke C	D	1-1	Graydon	28,492
21		13	(h)	Norwich C	W	3-2	Graydon, Deehan 2	30,478
22		20	(a)	Leeds U	L	0-1		29,118
23		26	(h)	West Ham U	W	4-1	Deehan 2, Hamilton, Gray	51,300
24		27	(a)	Derby Co	L	0-2		37,230
25	Jan	10	(a)	Arsenal	D	0-0		24,501
26		17	(h)	Newcastle U	D	1-1	Mahoney (og)	36,387
27		31	(h)	QPR	L	0-2		32,223
28	Feb	7	(a)	Manchester C	L	1-2	Gray	32,331
29		14	(a)	Sheffield U	L	1-2	Graydon	21,152
30		21	(h)	Manchester U	W	2-1	McDonald, Gray	50,094
31		24	(h)	Wolves	D	1-1	Graydon (pen)	47,693
32		28	(a)	Burnley	D	2-2	Graydon, Gray	17,123
33	Mar	6	(h)	Ipswich T	D	0-0		32,477
34		13	(a)	Tottenham H	L	2-5	Graydon, Gray	23,169
35		20	(a)	Leicester C	D	2-2	Nicholl 2	24,663
36		27	(h)	Stoke C	D	0-0		32,359
37	Apr	3	(a)	Birmingham C	L	2-3	Gray, Graydon (pen)	46,251
38		10	(h)	Liverpool	D	0-0		44,250
39		13	(a)	Coventry C	D	1-1	Nicholl	27,586
40		17	(a)	West Ham U	D	2-2	Deehan, Hunt	21,642
41		19	(h)	Derby Co	W	1-0	McDonald	39,241
42		24	(h)	Middlesbrough	W	2-1	Deehan, Carrodus	33,241

FINAL LEAGUE POSITION: 16th in Division One

Appearances

Sub. Appearances

Goals

Cumbes	Gidman	Aitken	Ross	Nicholl	Phillips	Graydon	Little B	Leonard	Hamilton	Carrodus	Deehan	Burridge	Cowans	Findlay	Gray	Hunt	Overton	Masefield	Mortimer	McDonald	Morgan	Pimblett	Robson							#
1	2	3	4	5	6	7	8	9	10	11																				1
1	2	3	4	5	6	7	8	9	10	11																				2
1	2	3	4	5	6	7	8	9	10	11																				3
1	2*	3	4	5	6	7	8	9	10	11												12								4
1		3	4	5	6	7	8	9	10	11												2								5
1		3	4	5	6	7	8	9*	10	11											12	2								6
1	2	3	4	5	6	7		9*	10											11	8	12								7
	2	3	4	5	6	7	8			11		1			12					9	10*									8
	2	3	4	5	6	7	8		10	11		1										9								9
	2	3	4	5	6	7	8		10	11		1										9								10
	2	3	6	5		7	8		10	11		1			9								4							11
	2	3	4	5	6	7	8		10	11		1			9															12
	2	3	4	5	6	7	8*		10	11		1			9							12								13
	2	3	4	5	6	7			10	11		1			9								8							14
	2	3	4	5	6	7			11	10		1			9				12				8							15
	2	3	4	5		7			11	10		1			9								6	8							16
	2	3	4	5	12	7			11	10		1			9								6*	8							17
	2		4	5	6	7			10	11	8	1			9								3							18
	2		4	5	6	7			10	11	8	1			9								3							19
	2		4	5	10	7			11	9	8	1			9							6	3							20
	2		4	5	6	7			10	11	8	1			9								3							21
		3	4	5	8	7			10*	11		1			9				12			6	2							22
	2		4	5		7			10	11	8	1			9					6			3							23
	2		4	5		7			10	11	8	1			9					6			3							24
	2	3	4	5	6				10	11		1			9					7			8							25
	2	3	4	5	12				11	7	10	1			9					6*			8							26
	2	3	4	5*	6	7			10	11	12	1			9								8							27
	2		4	5		7			10	11		1	12		9					6		8	3							28
	2		4	5	6	7			12	11	9*	1								10		8	3							29
	2		4	5	6	7	8			11		1			9					10			3							30
	2		4	5	6	7	8			11		1			9		12			10*			3							31
	2		4		6	7	8			11		1			9		5			10			3							32
	2		4	5	6	7	8*			11		1			9					10	12		3							33
	2		4	5	6	7	8		12	11		1			9					10			3							34
	2		4	5		7	8		10	11		1			9					6			3							35
	2		4	5		7	8		10	11		1			9					6			3							36
	2		4	5		7	8		10	11		1			9					6			3							37
	2		5	4	7				11					1	9	10				6	8		3							38
	2		5	4	7				11					1	9	10			12	6	8		3							39
	2		5	4					11	7				1	9	10				6	8		3							40
	2		5	4	7				11	10				1	9					6	8		3							41
	2		4	5		7			11	10				1	9					6	8		3							42
7	39	21	38	40	33	38	20	7	29	39	14	30		5	30	3	2		14	10	2	7	34							
				2		2		2		1		1			1	1	1		3	1		3								
		1		4	2	12	1	3	4	1	7				10	1				2										

33

1976-77

1	Aug	21	(h)	West Ham U	W	4-0	Gray 2, Graydon 2 (1 pen)	39,012
2		25	(a)	Manchester C	L	0-2		41,007
3		28	(a)	Everton	W	2-0	Little, Lyons (og)	32,058
4	Sep	4	(h)	Ipswich T	W	5-2	Little, Gray 3, Graydon	39,916
5		11	(a)	QPR	L	1-2	Gray	23,602
6		18	(h)	Birmingham C	L	1-2	Gray	50,084
7		25	(h)	Leicester C	W	2-0	Graydon (pen), Gray	36,652
8	Oct	2	(a)	Stoke C	L	0-1		29,652
9		16	(a)	Sunderland	W	1-0	Cropley	31,578
10		20	(h)	Arsenal	W	5-1	Mortimer, Graydon, Gray 2, Little	33,860
11		23	(h)	Bristol C	W	3-1	Nicholl, Gidman, Graydon	37,094
12		30	(a)	Liverpool	L	0-3		51,751
13	Nov	6	(h)	Manchester U	W	3-2	Mortimer, Gray 2	44,789
14		10	(a)	West Brom A	D	1-1	Mortimer	42,900
15		20	(h)	Coventry C	D	2-2	Gidman, Gray	40,047
16		27	(a)	Norwich C	D	1-1	Little	22,554
17	Dec	11	(a)	Leeds U	W	3-1	Gray 2, Cropley	31,232
18		15	(h)	Liverpool	W	5-1	Gray 2, Deehan 2, Little	42,851
19		18	(h)	Newcastle U	W	2-1	Deehan 2	33,982
20		27	(a)	Middlesbrough	L	2-3	Gray, Hughes	31,000
21	Jan	1	(a)	Manchester U	L	0-2		55,446
22		22	(a)	West Ham U	W	1-0	Gray	27,577
23	Feb	5	(h)	Everton	W	2-0	Gray, Little	41,305
24		12	(a)	Ipswich T	L	0-1		29,750
25	Mar	2	(h)	Derby Co	W	4-0	Mortimer, Gidman, Little, Cowans	37,396
26		5	(a)	Leicester C	D	1-1	Deehan	22,038
27		23	(h)	Sunderland	W	4-1	Gidman, Gray, Deehan 2	34,458
28	Apr	2	(a)	Bristol C	D	0-0		27,958
29		5	(h)	Middlesbrough	W	1-0	Deehan	32,646
30		9	(a)	Derby Co	L	1-2	Little	28,061
31		16	(a)	Coventry C	W	3-2	Cowans, Deehan, Little	31,158
32		20	(h)	Tottenham H	W	2-1	Little, Deehan	42,047
33		23	(h)	Norwich C	W	1-0	Little	35,899
34		25	(a)	Arsenal	L	0-3		23,961
35		30	(a)	Tottenham H	L	1-3	Deehan	30,890
36	May	4	(h)	Manchester C	D	1-1	Little	36,190
37		7	(h)	Leeds U	W	2-1	Deehan, Cropley	38,205
38		10	(a)	Birmingham C	L	1-2	Deehan	43,721
39		14	(a)	Newcastle U	L	2-3	Little 2	29,250
40		16	(h)	Stoke C	W	1-0	Gray (pen)	28,963
41		20	(h)	QPR	D	1-1	Cowans	28,056
42		23	(h)	West Brom A	W	4-0	Nicholl, Gray 3	42,542

FINAL LEAGUE POSITION: 4th in Division One

Appearances

Sub. Appearances

Goals

Burridge	Gidman	Smith	Phillips	Nichol	Mortimer	Graydon	Little	Gray	Robson	Carrodus	Cowans	Cropley	Deehan	Findlay	Hunt	Hughes	Linton	Masefield	Young	Buttress	
1	2	3	4	5	6	7	8	9	10	11											1
1	2	3	4	5	6	7	8	9	10	11											2
1	2	3	4	5	6	7	8	9	10	11											3
1	2	3	4	5	6	7	8	9	10	11											4
1	2	3	4	5	6	7	8	9	10*	11	12										5
1	2	3	4	5	6	7	8	9	10*	11					12						6
1	2	3	4	5	6	7	8	9		11		10									7
1	2	3	4	5	6	7	8	9		11		10									8
1	2	3	4	5	6	7	8	9		11		10									9
1	2	3	4	5	6	7	8	9		11		10									10
1	2	3	4	5	6	7	8	9		11		10									11
1	2	3	4	5	6	7	8	9		11		10									12
1	2	3	4	5	6	7	8	9		11		10									13
1	2	3	4	5	6	7*	8	9	12	11		10									14
	2	3	4	5	6		8	9		11		10	7	1							15
	2	3	4	5	6		8	9	7	11		10		1							16
	2		4		6		8	9	3	11		10	7	1				5			17
	2		4		6		8	9	3	11		10*	7	1				5	12		18
		2	4		6		8	9	3	11		10*	7	1				5	12		19
		2	4		6		8	9	3	11			7	1		10		5			20
1		2	4	5	6		8	9	3	11		10	7								21
1	2	12	4	5	6		8	9	3	11		10*	7								22
1	2		4	5	6		8	9*	3	11	12	10	7								23
1	2		4	5	6		8		3	11	9	10	7								24
1	2	12	4	5	6		8		3	11	9		7			10*					25
	2	10	4	5	6		8		3	11	9		7	1							26
1	2		4		6		8	9	3	11		10	7					5			27
1	2			5	6		8	9	3	11		10	7					4			28
1	2		4	5	6		8	9	3	11		10	7								29
1	2		4	5	6		8	9	3	11*	12	10	7								30
1	2		4	5	6	7	8		3			11	10	8							31
1	2		4	5*	6	7	8		3			11	10	9					12		32
1	2		4		6*	7	8		3			11	10	9		12		5			33
1	2		4				8	9	3	11		10	7			6*	12	5			34
1	2		4				8	9	3	11		10	7			6		5			35
1	2		4	5	6		8	9	3	11		10	7								36
1	2		4	5	6		8	9	3	11		10	7								37
1	2		4	5	6		8	9	3	11		10	7								38
1	2		4	5	6		8	9	3	10		11	7					4			39
1	2		4	5	6		8	9	3	11		10	7*				12				40
1	2		4	5	6		8	9	3	11		10	7								41
1	2		4	5	6		8	9*	3	11		10	7				12				42
35	27	32	40	34	40	17	42	36	33	30	16	32	27	7		4		10			
	2							1		3				1	1	2	1	1	2		
	4			2	4	6	14	25		3		3	13			1					

35

1977-78

1	Aug	20	(a)	QPR	W	2-1	Webb (og), Carrodus	25,431
2		24	(h)	Manchester C	L	1-4	Deehan	40,121
3		27	(h)	Everton	L	1-2	Gray	37,806
4	Sep	3	(a)	Bristol C	D	1-1	Little	22,200
5		10	(h)	Arsenal	W	1-0	Cropley	36,929
6		17	(a)	Nottingham F	L	0-2		31,016
7		23	(h)	Wolves	W	2-0	Brazier (og), Deehan	40,403
8	Oct	1	(h)	Birmingham C	L	0-1		45,436
9		5	(a)	Leeds U	D	1-1	Gray	27,797
10		8	(a)	Leicester C	W	2-0	Cowans, Gray	20,276
11		15	(h)	Norwich C	W	3-0	Gray, Cowans, Little	32,978
12		22	(a)	West Ham U	D	2-2	McNaught, Gray	26,599
13		29	(h)	Manchester U	W	2-1	Gray, Cropley	39,144
14	Nov	5	(a)	Liverpool	W	2-1	Gray 2	50,436
15		12	(h)	Middlesbrough	L	0-1		31,837
16		19	(a)	Chelsea	D	0-0		31,764
17	Dec	3	(a)	Ipswich T	L	0-2		20,917
18		10	(h)	West Brom A	W	3-0	Cowans, Gray, Gidman	41,631
19		17	(a)	Middlesbrough	L	0-1		14,999
20		26	(h)	Coventry C	D	1-1	Deehan	43,571
21		27	(a)	Derby Co	W	3-0	Little, Gray, Deehan	30,395
22		31	(a)	Manchester C	L	0-2		46,074
23	Jan	2	(h)	QPR	D	1-1	Little	34,750
24		14	(a)	Everton	L	0-1		40,630
25		28	(h)	Bristol C	W	1-0	Deehan	29,676
26	Feb	4	(a)	Arsenal	W	1-0	MacDonald (og)	30,127
27		25	(a)	Birmingham C	L	0-1		33,679
28	Mar	4	(h)	Leicester C	D	0-0		29,971
29		11	(a)	Norwich C	L	1-2	Gregory	19,031
30		18	(h)	West Ham U	W	4-1	Gregory 2, Deehan, Mortimer	28,275
31		21	(a)	Coventry C	W	3-2	Little, McNaught, Gray	30,957
32		25	(h)	Derby Co	D	0-0		32,793
33		29	(a)	Manchester U	D	1-1	Deehan	41,625
34	Apr	1	(h)	Liverpool	L	0-3		40,190
35		5	(h)	Nottingham F	L	0-1		44,215
36		8	(a)	Newcastle U	D	1-1	Evans A	17,203
37		15	(h)	Chelsea	W	2-0	Cowans, Wicks (og)	27,375
38		17	(h)	Newcastle U	W	2-0	Cowans, Gray	25,493
39		22	(a)	West Brom A	W	3-0	Deehan, Cowans, Mortimer	35,000
40		26	(h)	Leeds U	W	3-1	Deehan, Mortimer, Little	30,524
41		29	(h)	Ipswich T	W	6-1	Deehan 2, Gray, Little, Carrodus, Cowans	30,955
42	May	2	(a)	Wolves	L	1-3	Carrodus	30,644

FINAL LEAGUE POSITION: 8th in Division One

Appearances

Sub. Appearances

Goals

Rimmer	Gregory	Smith	Phillips	McNaught	Mortimer	Deehan	Little	Cowans	Cropley	Carrodus	Craig	Linton	Evans A	Gray	Gidman	Robson	Buttress	
1	2	3	4	5	6	7	8	9	10	11								1
1	2	3	4	5	6	7	8		10	11				9				2
1	2	3	4	5	6	7	8	12	10	11				9*				3
1	2		4	5	6	7	8		10	11				9		3		4
1			4	5	6	7	8		10	11				9	2	3		5
1			4	5	6	7	8	9	10	11					2	3		6
1		3	4	5	6	7	8	9	10	11					2			7
1	4	3	5		6	7	8*	9	10	11				12	2			8
1		3	4	5	6	7		8	10	11				9	2			9
1		3	4	5	6	7		8	10	11				9	2			10
1		3	4	5	6	7*	8	12	10	11				9	2			11
1		3	4	5	6	7*	8	12	10	11				9	2			12
1		3	4	5	6	7	8		10	11				9	2			13
1		3	4	5	6		8	7	10	11				9	2			14
1		3	4	5	6		8	7	10	11				9	2			15
1		3	4	5	6	7	8		10	11				9	2			16
1	10	3	4	5	6		8	7		11				9	2			17
1	7	3	4	5*	6		8	12	10	11				9	2			18
1	7	3	4	5	6		8	10		11				9	2			19
1	2	3	4	5	6	7	8	10		11				9				20
1	10	3	4	5	6	7	8	12		11*				9	2			21
1	10	3	4	5	6	7	8			11				9	2			22
1	10	3	4	5	6	7	8	11						9	2			23
1	4	3		5	6	7	8	10				12		9*	2		11	24
1		3	4	5	6	7	8	9		11	10				2			25
1	2	3	4	5	6	9	8	10		11	7							26
1	12	3	4	5	6	9	8	10		11	7			2*				27
1	2	3	4	5	6	9	8	10		11	7							28
1	12	3	4	5	6	9	8			11	7		10*		2			29
1	7	3	4	5	6	9	8	10		11					2			30
1	7	3	4	5	6		8	10		11				9	2			31
1	7	3	4	5	6	12	8	10*		11				9	2			32
1		3	4	5	6	7	8	10		11				9	2			33
1	12	3	4	5	6	7	8	10		11*				9	2			34
1		3	4	5	6	7	8	10		11				9	2			35
1	2	3	4	5	6	7	8	10		11				9				36
1		3		5	6	7	8	10		11			4	9	2			37
1	12	3		5*	6	7	8	10		11			4	9	2			38
1	5	3			6	7	8	10		11			4	9	2			39
1		3		5	6	7	8	10		11			4	9	2			40
1		3		5	6	7	8	10		11			4	9	2			41
1	12	3		5	6	7	8	10		11			4	9*	2			42
42	21	38	35	40	42	35	40	30	17	40	4		9	31	34	3	1	
	5					1		5				1		1				
	3			2	3	11	7	7	2	3			1	13	1			

1978-79

1	Aug	19	(h)	Wolves	W	1-0	Gray	43,922
2		23	(a)	Tottenham H	W	4-1	Evans A, Gregory, Little, Shelton	47,892
3		26	(a)	Bristol C	L	0-1		23,493
4	Sep	2	(h)	Southampton	D	1-1	Gray	34,067
5		9	(a)	Ipswich T	W	2-0	Gregory, Gray (pen)	22,166
6		16	(h)	Everton	D	1-1	Craig	38,636
7		23	(a)	QPR	L	0-1		16,410
8		30	(h)	Nottingham F	L	1-2	Craig (pen)	36,735
9	Oct	7	(a)	Arsenal	D	1-1	Gregory	34,537
10		14	(h)	Manchester U	D	2-2	Gregory 2	36,204
11		21	(a)	Birmingham C	W	1-0	Gray	36,145
12		27	(h)	Middlesbrough	L	0-2		36,615
13	Nov	4	(h)	Manchester C	D	1-1	Deehan	32,724
14		11	(a)	Wolves	W	4-0	Shelton, McNaught, Deehan, Mortimer	23,289
15		18	(h)	Bristol C	W	2-0	Deehan, Cowans	27,621
16		21	(a)	Southampton	L	0-2		20,880
17		25	(a)	West Brom A	D	1-1	Evans A	35,085
18	Dec	9	(a)	Chelsea	W	1-0	Evans A	19,080
19		16	(h)	Norwich C	D	1-1	McGuire (og)	26,238
20		23	(a)	Derby Co	D	0-0		20,109
21		26	(h)	Leeds U	D	2-2	Gregory 2	40,973
22	Jan	31	(a)	Everton	D	1-1	Shelton	29,079
23	Feb	24	(a)	Manchester U	D	1-1	Swain	44,437
24	Mar	3	(h)	Birmingham C	W	1-0	Cowans	42,419
25		7	(h)	Bolton W	W	3-0	Gray, Swain, Jones (og)	28,053
26		10	(a)	Middlesbrough	L	0-2		16,562
27		20	(h)	QPR	W	3-1	Evans A, Gidman (pen), Mortimer	24,310
28		24	(a)	Tottenham H	L	2-3	Gidman, (pen), Gray	35,486
29		28	(h)	Coventry C	D	1-1	Evans A	25,670
30	Apr	4	(a)	Nottingham F	L	0-4		27,056
31		7	(a)	Coventry C	D	1-1	Deehan	23,690
32		11	(h)	Derby Co	D	3-3	Cowans 2, Gidman (pen)	21,884
33		14	(a)	Leeds U	L	0-1		24,281
34		16	(h)	Liverpool	W	3-1	Evans A, Thompson (og), Deehan	44,029
35		21	(a)	Norwich C	W	2-1	Shelton, Cropley	15,061
36		25	(h)	Arsenal	W	5-1	Shelton 3 (1 pen), Deehan 2	26,168
37		28	(h)	Chelsea	W	2-1	Wilkins (og), Swain	29,219
38	May	2	(h)	Ipswich T	D	2-2	Swain, Deehan	26,636
39		5	(a)	Bolton W	D	0-0		17,394
40		8	(a)	Liverpool	L	0-3		50,570
41		11	(h)	West Brom A	L	0-1		35,991
42		15	(a)	Manchester C	W	3-2	Cropley, Mortimer, Deehan	30,028

FINAL LEAGUE POSITION: 8th in Division One

Appearances

Sub. Appearances

Goals

Rimmer	Gidman	Smith	Evans A	McNaught	Mortimer	Shelton	Little	Gray	Cowans	Carrodus	Gregory	Craig	Deehan	Evans D	Gibson	Cropley	Jenkins	Linton	Ormsby	Phillips	Shaw	Swain	Williams	Ward	Young	
1	2	3	4	5	6	7	8	9*	10	11	12															1
1	2	3	4	5	6	7	8		10	11	9															2
1	2	3	4	5	6	7*	8		10	11	9									12						3
1	2	3	4	5	6	7	8	9	10	11																4
1	2*	3	4	5	6		8	9	10		11	7				12										5
1			4	5	6	11*	8	9	10		3	7		2									12			6
1			4	5	6	11	8		10		3	7	9*	2						12						7
1			4	5	6	11	8		10*		2	7	9			12							3			8
1			4	5	6		8			11	2	7	9								10		3			9
1	2			5				9		11	6	7	8						4				3		10	10
1	2		4	5	6		8	9			10	7											3		11	11
1	2		4	5	6		8	9			10	7								12			3		11*	12
1	2*	12		5	6		8	9			11	7	10						4				3			13
1	2		4	5	6	7	8		10		11		9										3			14
1	2		4*	5	6	7			10		11		9		12		8						3			15
1	2*	12	4	5	6	7			10		11		9				8						3			16
1	2		4	5	6				10		11	7	9								8		3			17
1	2	3	4	5	6				10		11	7	9			12					8*					18
1	2		4	5	6				10		11	7	8									9	3			19
1	2		4	5	6	11			10			7	8									9	3			20
1	2		4	5	6				10		11	7	9									8	3			21
1	2		9	5	6	11*			10		4	7				12						8	3			22
1	2			5	6	11			10		4	7										8	3	9		23
1	2			5	6		8	9	10		4	7										11	3			24
1	2			5	6		8	9*	10		4	7	12			6						11	3			25
1				5			8	9	10		4	7				6		2				11	3			26
1	2			5	6		8*	9	10		4	7				12						11	3			27
1	2			5	6		8	9	10		4	7										11	3			28
1				5	6		8	9	10		4	7						2				11	3			29
1	2		4	5	6		8	9			3	7				10						11				30
1	2		4	5	6		8	7			3		9			10						11				31
1	2			5	6*		8	7					9		3	10		4				11	12			32
1	2		4	5			8	7			6		9		3	10						11				33
1	2		4	5	6			7			8		9		3	10						11				34
1	2		5*	6	7		8				4		9		3	10	12					11				35
1	2			6	8			7			4		9		3	10		5				11				36
1	2		5		6	8		7			4		9		3	10						11				37
1	2		5		6	8		7			4		9		3	10						11				38
1	2		8	5	6			7			4		9		3	10						11				39
1	2		8	5	6			7			4		9		3	10*	12					11				40
1	2		4*	5	6	7					8		9		3	10	12					11				41
1	2			5	6	7	8				4		9		3	10						11				42
42	36	6	36	32	38	19	24	15	34	6	38	23	25	2	11	15		4	2	3	2	24	21	1	3	
	1	1									1		1		1	2	2	4	2		1		2			
	3		6	1	3	7	1	6	4		7	2	9			2						4				

1979-80

1	Aug	18	(a)	Bolton W	D	1-1	Cowans	19,795
2		22	(h)	Brighton & HA	W	2-1	Evans A (pen), Morley	28,803
3		25	(h)	Bristol C	L	0-2		25,526
4	Sep	1	(a)	Everton	D	1-1	Morley	29,271
5		8	(h)	Manchester U	L	0-3		34,859
6		15	(a)	Crystal P	L	0-2		28,156
7		22	(h)	Arsenal	D	0-0		27,277
8		29	(a)	Middlesbrough	D	0-0		16,017
9	Oct	6	(h)	Southampton	W	3-0	Bremner, Mortimer, Evans A (pen)	24,377
10		13	(h)	West Brom A	D	0-0		36,007
11		20	(a)	Derby C	W	3-1	Little, Shaw, Mortimer	20,152
12		27	(a)	Wolves	D	1-1	Shaw	36,267
13	Nov	3	(h)	Bolton W	W	3-1	Shaw, A. Evans, Mortimer	24,744
14		10	(a)	Ipswich T	D	0-0		17,807
15		17	(h)	Stoke C	W	2-1	Mortimer, Evans A (pen)	27,086
16		24	(h)	Leeds U	D	0-0		29,736
17	Dec	1	(a)	Norwich C	D	1-1	Evans A	15,885
18		8	(h)	Liverpool	L	1-3	Little	41,160
19		15	(a)	Tottenham H	W	2-1	Geddis, Cowans (pen)	30,555
20		19	(h)	Coventry C	W	3-0	Donovan, Little 2	24,446
21		26	(a)	Nottingham F	L	1-2	Shaw	30,979
22		29	(a)	Bristol C	W	3-1	Shaw 3	18,221
23	Jan	12	(h)	Everton	W	2-1	Gibson, Donovan	31,108
24	Feb	2	(h)	Crystal P	W	2-0	Cowans, Mortimer	29,469
25		9	(a)	Arsenal	L	1-3	Mortimer	33,816
26		23	(a)	West Brom A	W	2-1	McNaught, Little	33,658
27		27	(h)	Manchester C	D	2-2	Shaw, Donachie (og)	29,139
28	Mar	1	(h)	Derby C	W	1-0	Evans A	28,956
29		3	(a)	Brighton & HA	D	1-1	Evans A	23,077
30		10	(h)	Wolves	L	1-3	Shaw	30,432
31		15	(a)	Southampton	L	0-2		20,735
32		19	(h)	Middlesbrough	L	0-2		15,319
33		22	(h)	Ipswich T	D	1-1	Morley	22,386
34		26	(h)	Norwich C	W	2-0	Cowans (pen), Hopkins	17,956
35		29	(a)	Stoke C	L	0-2		16,234
36	Apr	5	(h)	Nottingham F	W	3-2	Bremner, Evans A, Lloyd (og)	29,156
37		7	(a)	Manchester C	D	1-1	Geddis	42,584
38		19	(a)	Leeds U	D	0-0		15,840
39		23	(a)	Manchester U	L	1-2	Bremner	45,201
40		26	(h)	Tottenham H	W	1-0	Cowans	29,549
41		29	(a)	Coventry C	W	2-1	Gibson, Cowans (pen)	17,969
42	May	3	(a)	Liverpool	L	1-4	Cohen (og)	51,451

FINAL LEAGUE POSITION: 7th in Division One

Appearances

Sub. Appearances

Goals

Rimmer	Swain	Gibson	Evans A	McNaught	Mortimer	Morley	Little	Deehan	Cowans	Shelton	Bremner	Bullivant	Balke	Cropley	Deacy	Donovan	Gidman	Geddis	Hopkins	Heard	Jenkins	Linton	Ormsby	Pejic	Shaw	Spink	Williams	Ward	
1	2	3	4	5	6	7	8	9	10	11																			1
1	2	3	4	5		7	8	9	10	11				6*									12						2
1	2	3	4	5		7	8*	9	10	11													12				6		3
1	11	3	4	5	6	7		9	10														2		8				4
1	11		4	5	6	7		9	10	3*							2								8		12		5
1	11		4	5	6	7		9	10								2						12	3			8*		6
1	11		4	5	6		8		10		7						2	9						3					7
1	11		4	5	6		8		10		7						2*	9						3			12		8
1	11	2	4				8		10		7							9					5	3					9
1	2		4		6		8		10		7							9					5	3	11				10
1	2		4		6		8		10		7							9					5	3	11				11
1	2	3	4		6		8		10		7							9					5		11				12
1	2	3	4	5	6		8		10		7							9							11				13
1	2	3	4	5	6		8		10		7							9							11				14
1	2		4	5	6		8		10		7							9						3	11				15
1	2		4	5	6		8		10		7							9						3	11				16
1	2		4	5	6		8		10		7							9						3	11				17
1	2	12	4	5			8		10		7	6*						9						3	11				18
1	2	3		5			8		10		7	6		12				9*					4		11				19
1	2	3		5			8		10		7	6				9							4		11				20
	2	3		5			8		10		7	6				9							4		11	1			21
1	2	3		5			8		10		7					9							4		11				22
1	2	3	4	5	6		8		10		7					9									11				23
1	2	3	4	5	6		8		10		7					9									11				24
1	2	3	4	5	6		8		10		7					9		12							11*				25
1	2	3	4	5	6	7	8		10		9														11				26
1	2	3	4	5	6	7	8		10		9														11				27
1	2	3	4	5	6	7	8		10		9														11				28
1	2*	3	4	5	6		8		10		7	11				9							12						29
1		3	9	5	6		8		10		7											2	4		11				30
1	2	3	8	5	6	9			10		7											12	4		11*				31
1	2	3	5			11			10		7	6				9		8*				12	4						32
1	8	3	9	5		11			10		7	6										2	4						33
1	8	3	9	5		11			10		7								12	6		2*	4						34
1	8	3	9	5		11*			10		7								12	6		2	4						35
1	2	3	4						10		7					9		8		6		11	5						36
1	2	3	4			9			10		7							8		6		11	5						37
1	2		4			12	8*		10		7				3					6		9	5		11				38
1	2		4			12	8		10		7				3*					6		9	5		11				39
1	2	3							10		7		4					9		6		11	5		8				40
1	2	3							10		7		4					9		6		11	5		8				41
1	2	3				12			10		7		4					9		6		11*	5		8				42
41	41	30	35	30	26	15	29	6	42	4	36	6	3	1	2	9	4	19		9		12	21	10	28	1	1	1	
		1				3									1			1	2		1	3	2				1	1	
		2	8	1	6	3	5				6	3				2		2	1						9				

41

1980-81

1	Aug	16	(a)	Leeds U	W	2-1	Morley, Shaw	23,401
2		20	(h)	Norwich C	W	1-0	Shaw	25,970
3		23	(a)	Manchester C	D	2-2	Withe 2	30,017
4		30	(h)	Coventry C	W	1-0	Shaw	20,050
5	Sep	6	(a)	Ipswich T	L	0-1		23,192
6		13	(h)	Everton	L	0-2		25,673
7		20	(h)	Wolves	W	2-1	Hughes (og), Geddis	26,881
8		27	(a)	Crystal P	W	1-0	Shaw	18,398
9	Oct	4	(h)	Sunderland	W	4-0	Evans 2, Morley, Shaw	26,194
10		8	(a)	Manchester U	D	3-3	Withe, Cowans (pen), Shaw	38,831
11		11	(a)	Birmingham C	W	2-1	Cowans (pen), Evans	33,879
12		18	(a)	Tottenham H	W	3-0	Morley 2, Withe	30,940
13		22	(h)	Brighton & HA	W	4-1	Mortimer, Withe, Bremmer, Shaw	27,367
14		25	(a)	Southampton	W	2-1	Morley, Withe	21,249
15	Nov	1	(h)	Leicester C	W	2-0	Shaw, Cowans	29,953
16		8	(a)	West Brom A	D	0-0		34,001
17		12	(a)	Norwich C	W	3-1	Shaw 2, Evans	17,050
18		15	(h)	Leeds U	D	1-1	Shaw	29,106
19		22	(a)	Liverpool	L	1-2	Evans	48,114
20		29	(h)	Arsenal	D	1-1	Morley	30,140
21	Dec	6	(a)	Middlesbrough	L	1-2	Shaw	15,597
22		13	(h)	Birmingham C	W	3-0	Geddis 2, Shaw	41,101
23		20	(a)	Brighton & HA	L	0-1		16,425
24		26	(h)	Stoke C	W	1-0	Withe	34,658
25		27	(a)	Nottingham F	D	2-2	Lloyd (og), Shaw	33,390
26	Jan	10	(h)	Liverpool	W	2-0	Withe, Mortimer	47,960
27		17	(a)	Coventry C	W	2-1	Morley, Withe	27,020
28		31	(h)	Manchester C	W	1-0	Shaw	33,682
29	Feb	7	(a)	Everton	W	3-1	Morley, Mortimer, Cowans (pen)	31,434
30		21	(h)	Crystal P	W	2-1	Withe 2	27,203
31		28	(a)	Wolves	W	1-0	Withe	34,693
32	Mar	7	(a)	Sunderland	W	2-1	Evans, Mortimer	27,278
33		14	(h)	Manchester U	D	3-3	Withe 2, Shaw	42,182
34		21	(a)	Tottenham H	L	0-2		35,091
35		28	(h)	Southampton	W	2-1	Morley, Geddis	32,467
36	Apr	4	(a)	Leicester C	W	4-2	Withe 2, Bremner, Morley	26,032
37		8	(h)	West Brom A	W	1-0	Withe	47,998
38		14	(h)	Ipswich T	L	1-2	Shaw	47,495
39		18	(h)	Nottingham F	W	2-0	Cowans (pen), Withe	34,707
40		20	(a)	Stoke C	D	1-1	Withe	23,500
41		25	(h)	Middlesbrough	W	3-0	Shaw, Withe, Evans	38,018
42	May	2	(a)	Arsenal	L	0-2		57,472

FINAL LEAGUE POSITION: Champions of Division One

Appearances

Sub. Appearances

Goals

Rimmer	Swain	Deacy	Williams	McNaught	Mortimer	Bremner	Shaw	Withe	Cowans	Morley	Evans	Gibson	Geddis	
1	2	3	4	5	6	7	8	9	10	11				1
1	2			5	6	7	8	9	10	11	4	3		2
1	2			5	6	7	8	9	10	11	4	3		3
1	2			5	6	7	8	9	10	11	4	3		4
1	2			5	6	7	8	9	10	11	4	3		5
1	2			5	6	7	8	9	10	11	4	3		6
1	2			5	6	7		9	10	11	4	3	8	7
1	2			5	6	7	8	9	10	11	4	3		8
1	2			5	6	7	8	9	10	11	4	3		9
1	2	3		5	6	7	8	9	10	11	4			10
1	2	3		5	6	7	8	9	10	11	4			11
1	2			5	6	7	8	9	10	11	4	3		12
1	2			5	6	7	8	9	10	11	4	3		13
1	2	12		5	6	7	8	9	10	11*	4	3		14
1	2	3*	12	5	6	7	8	9	10	11	4			15
1	2	3		5	6	7	8	9	10	11	4			16
1	2	3		5	6	7	8	9	10	11	4			17
1	2	3		5	6	7	8	9	10	11	4			18
1	2	3		5	6	7	8	9	10	11	4			19
1	2	3		5	6	7	8	9	10	11	4			20
1	2	3		5	6	7	8		10	11	4	9		21
1	2	3		5	6	7	8		10	11	4	9		22
1	2	12	3	5	6	7	8		10	11	4	9*		23
1	2	3		5	6	7	8	9	10	11	4			24
1	2	3		5	6	7	8		10	11	4	9		25
1	2			5	6	7	8	9	10	11	4	3		26
1	2			5	6	7	8	9	10	11	4	3		27
1	2	3	5*		6	7	8	9	10	11	4	12		28
1	2	3		5	6	7	8	9	10	11	4			29
1	2		3*	5	6	7	8	9	10	11	4	12		30
1	2	3		5	6	7	8	9	10	11	4			31
1	2	3	5*		6	7	8	9	10	11	4	12		32
1	2	3		5	6	7	8	9	10	11	4			33
1	2	3		5	6	7	8		10	11	4	9		34
1	2	3		5	6	7	8		10	11	4	9		35
1	2	3		5	6	7	8	9	10	11	4			36
1	2			5	6	7		9	10	11	4	3	8	37
1	2		4	5	6	7	8	9	10	11		3		38
1	2		4	5	6	7	8	9	10	11		3		39
1	2	12		5	6	7	8	9	10	11	4	3		40
1	2			5	6	7	8	9	10	11	4	3		41
1	2			5	6	7	8	9	10	11	4	3		42
42	42	5	21	42	42	42	40	36	42	42	39	19	8	
		3	1									2	1	
				4	2	18	20	5	10	7			4	

43

1981-82

								Attendance
1	Aug	29	(h)	Notts Co	L	0-1		30,097
2	Sep	2	(a)	Sunderland	L	1-2	Donovan	29,372
3		5	(a)	Tottenham H	W	3-1	Donovan 2, Mortimer	31,265
4		12	(h)	Manchester U	D	1-1	Cowans	37,661
5		19	(a)	Liverpool	D	0-0		37,474
6		23	(h)	Stoke C	D	2-2	Withe 2	25,637
7		26	(h)	Birmingham C	D	0-0		40,763
8	Oct	3	(a)	Leeds U	D	1-1	Shaw	21,065
9		10	(a)	Coventry C	D	1-1	Shaw	16,306
10		17	(h)	West Ham U	W	3-2	Morley, Geddis, Mortimer	32,064
11		24	(a)	Wolves	W	3-0	Shaw 2, Palmer (og)	19,942
12		31	(h)	Ipswich T	L	0-1		32,652
13	Nov	7	(h)	Arsenal	L	0-2		27,316
14		21	(a)	Middlesbrough	D	3-3	Withe, Cowans, Shaw	12,522
15		28	(h)	Nottingham F	W	3-1	Bremner 2, Withe	26,847
16	Dec	5	(a)	Manchester C	L	0-1		32,487
17		15	(a)	Swansea C	L	1-2	Thompson (og)	15,191
18		19	(a)	Everton	L	0-2		16,538
19		28	(a)	Brighton & HA	W	1-0	Morley	24,287
20	Jan	16	(a)	Notts Co	L	0-1		9,597
21		30	(h)	Liverpool	L	0-3		35,947
22	Feb	2	(h)	Sunderland	W	1-0	Geddis	19,916
23		6	(a)	Manchester U	L	1-4	Geddis	43,184
24		10	(h)	Southampton	D	1-1	Withe	24,287
25		17	(h)	Tottenham H	D	1-1	Withe	23,877
26		20	(a)	Birmingham C	W	1-0	Withe	32,779
27		27	(h)	Coventry C	W	2-1	Cowans (pen), Shaw	24,474
28	Mar	6	(a)	West Ham U	D	2-2	Cowans, Withe	26,894
29		13	(h)	Wolves	W	3-1	Donovan, Morley, Shaw	26,790
30		20	(a)	Ipswich T	L	1-3	McNaught	20,407
31		27	(a)	Arsenal	L	3-4	Shaw, Morley, Heard	24,756
32		30	(h)	West Brom A	W	2-1	Shaw, Withe	28,440
33	Apr	10	(a)	Southampton	W	3-0	Nicholl (og), McNaught, Morley	22,801
34		12	(h)	Brighton & HA	W	3-0	Geddis 2, Evans	22,731
35		17	(h)	Middlesbrough	W	1-0	Evans	21,098
36		24	(a)	Nottingham F	D	1-1	Cowans (pen)	18,213
37		28	(h)	Leeds U	L	1-4	Geddis	20,566
38	May	1	(h)	Manchester C	D	0-0		22,150
39		5	(a)	Stoke C	L	0-1		10,363
40		8	(a)	West Brom A	W	1-0	Heard	19,615
41		15	(h)	Everton	L	1-2	Cowans	20,446
42		21	(h)	Swansea C	W	3-0	Morley, Bremner, Withe	18,294

FINAL LEAGUE POSITION: 11th in Division One

Appearances

Sub. Appearances

Goals

44

Rimmer	Swain	Gibson	Evans	McNaught	Mortimer	Bremner	Geddis	Withe	Cowans	Morley	Blair	Blake	Bullivant	Donovan	Deacy	Heard	Jones	Linton	Ormsby	Shaw	Shelton	Williams	Walters	
1	2	3	4	5*	6	7	8	9	10	11	12													1
1	2	3	4		6	7		9	10	11			8						5					2
1	2	3	4		6	7		9	10	11			8						5					3
1	2	3	4		6	7		9	10	11			8						5					4
1	2	3	4	5	6	7		9	10	11			8											5
1	2	3	4	5*	6	7		9	10	11	12		8											6
1	2	3	4		6	7		9	10	11			8						5					7
1	2	3	4		6	7		9	10	11									5	8*				8
1	2	3	4		6	7		9	10	11									5	8				9
1		3	4		6	7		9*	10	11	12								5	8		2		10
1		3	4		6	7		9	10	11									5	8		2		11
1	2	3	4		6	7		9	10	11									5	8				12
1	2	3	4		6	7		9	10	11	12									8		5		13
1	2	3	4			7		9	10	11					6					8		5		14
1	2	3	4			7		9	10	11					6					8		5		15
1	2	3	4			7		9	10	11					6					8		5		16
1	2	3	4			7		9	10	11					6*		12			8		5		17
1	2	3	4			7		9	10	11		5	6	8										18
1	2	3	4		6	7		9	10	11										8		5		19
1	2	3	4		6	7		9	10	11										8		5		20
1	2	3	4		6	7	8	9	10	11	12											5*		21
1	2	3*			6	7	8	9	10	4			12						5		11			22
1	2	3	4		6	7	8	9	10	11			5											23
1	2		4	5	6	7	8	9	10	11												3		24
1	2		4	5	6	7		9	10											8		3		25
1	2		4	5	6	7		9	10	11	12									8		3		26
1		4*	5		6	7		9	10	11	12						2			8		3		27
1	2		5	6	4			9	10	11						7				8		3		28
1	2		4	5	6	7			10	11				9						8		3		29
1	2		4	5					10	11	7*		6	9		12				8		3		30
1	2		4	5				9	10	11			7			6				8		3		31
1	2		4	5	6			9	10	11						7				8		3		32
1	2		4	5	6	7		9	10	11										8		3		33
1	2		4	5	6	7	8	9	10	11						12						3*		34
1	2		4	5			8	9	10	11	7					6						3		35
1	2		4	5	6*	7		9	10	11	12									8		3		36
1	2			5	7		8	9	10	11*						6		12	4			3		37
1	2			5	7			9	10	11						6			4	8		3		38
1	2		4	5	6	7		9	10	11	12									8		3		39
1	2		4	5	6	7		9	10							11				8		3		40
1	2		4	5	6	7		9	10		12					11				8*		3		41
1	2		4	5	6	7	8*	9	10	11						12						3		42
42	39	23	38	22	32	38	14	35	42	36	9	1	4	8	4	6	2		12	26	1	28		
										1	9		2			3		1				-1		
			2	2	2	3	6	10	6	6			4			2				9				

45

1982-83

1	Aug	28	(h)	Sunderland	L	1-3	Cowans	22,945
2		31	(a)	Everton	L	0-5		24,026
3	Sep	4	(a)	Southampton	L	0-1		17,943
4		8	(h)	Luton T	W	4-1	Mortimer, Withe, Cowans 2 (2 pens)	18,823
5		11	(h)	Nottingham F	W	4-1	Mortimer, Withe 2, Cowans (pen)	21,224
6		18	(a)	Manchester C	W	1-0	Shaw	28,650
7		25	(h)	Swansea C	W	2-0	Mortimer, Evans	21,246
8	Oct	2	(a)	West Brom A	L	0-1		25,300
9		9	(a)	Notts Co	L	1-4	Shaw	8,990
10		16	(h)	Watford	W	3-0	Withe, Morley 2	21,572
11		23	(a)	Norwich C	L	0-1		15,761
12		30	(h)	Tottenham H	W	4-0	Cowans 2 (1 pen), Morley, Shaw	25,992
13	Nov	6	(a)	Coventry C	D	0-0		12,076
14		13	(h)	Brighton & HA	W	1-0	Withe	18,834
15		20	(h)	Manchester U	W	2-1	Shaw, Withe	35,487
16		27	(a)	Stoke C	W	3-0	Parkin (og), Shaw 2	18,886
17	Dec	4	(h)	West Ham U	W	1-0	Cowans (pen)	24,658
18		7	(a)	Arsenal	L	1-2	McNaught	17,384
19		18	(h)	Liverpool	L	2-4	Shaw, Withe	34,568
20		27	(a)	Birmingham C	L	0-3		43,864
21		29	(h)	Ipswich T	D	1-1	Withe	21,912
22	Jan	1	(a)	Manchester U	L	1-3	Cowans (pen)	41,545
23		3	(h)	Southampton	W	2-0	Cowans (pen), Evans	19,925
24		15	(a)	Sunderland	L	0-2		16,052
25		22	(h)	Manchester C	D	1-1	Shaw	20,415
26	Feb	5	(a)	Nottingham F	W	2-1	Withe 2	16,352
27		12	(h)	Everton	W	2-0	Morley, Withe	21,117
28		26	(a)	Watford	L	1-2	Walters	19,318
29	Mar	5	(h)	Norwich C	W	3-2	Withe, Deacy, Shaw	18,624
30		8	(h)	Notts Co	W	2-0	Withe, Shaw	17,452
31		19	(h)	Coventry C	W	4-0	Shaw, Withe 2, Evans	20,509
32		23	(a)	Tottenham H	L	0-2		22,455
33		26	(a)	Brighton & HA	D	0-0		14,657
34	Apr	2	(a)	Ipswich T	W	2-1	Shaw, Withe	19,912
35		4	(h)	Birmingham C	W	1-0	Shaw	40,897
36		9	(a)	Luton T	L	1-2	Shaw	10,924
37		19	(h)	West Brom A	W	1-0	Mortimer	26,921
38		23	(a)	West Ham U	L	0-2		21,822
39		30	(h)	Stoke C	W	4-0	Cowans, McNaught, Morley, Evans	20,944
40	May	2	(a)	Swansea C	L	1-2	Shaw	9,173
41		7	(a)	Liverpool	D	1-1	Shaw (pen)	39,939
42		14	(h)	Arsenal	W	1-2	Shaw, Gibson	24,647

FINAL LEAGUE POSITION: 6th in Division One

Appearances

Sub. Appearances

Goals

Rimmer	Swain	Williams	Evans	McNaught	Mortimer	Bremner	Walters	Withe	Cowans	Morley	Heard	Blair	Hopkins	Jones	Shaw	Curbishley	Deacy	Geddis	Gibson	Spink	Walker	
1	2	3	4	5	6	7	8	9*	10	11	12											1
1	2	3	4*	5	6	7		9	10	11	12				8							2
1				5	6	4		9	10	11	3	7		2				8				3
1				5	6	4	12	9	10	11	3	7		2	8*							4
1		2	12	5	6	4		9	10	11	3	7			8*							5
1		3	4	5	6	7		9	10	11				2	8							6
1		3	4	5	6	7		9	10	11				2	8							7
1		3	4	5	6	7		9	10	11				2	8							8
1		3*	4		6	5		9	10	12	11		7	2	8							9
1			4	5	6	7		9	10	11				2	8				3			10
1		12	4*	5	6	7			10	11				2	8			9	3			11
1		2	4	5	6	7		9	10	11					8				3			12
1		3	4	5	6	7		9	10	11					8		2					13
1		3	4	5	6	7	12	9	10	11					8		2					14
1		3	4	5	6	7		9	10	11				2	8*							15
1		3	4	5	6	7		9	10	11				2	8							16
1		3	4	5	6*	7	12	9	10	11				2	8							17
1		3	4	5		7	12	9	10	11	6*			2	8							18
1		3	4	5	6	7	11	9	10					2	8							19
1		3	4	5	6	7	11	9	10					2	8							20
		2*	4	5	6	7	11	9	10	12					8				3	1		21
		2	4	5	6	7	11	9	10						8				3	1		22
		3	4	5	6	7		9	10	11				2	8					1		23
		3	4	5	6	7	8	9	10	11				2	8					1		24
		2	4	5	6	7		9	10	11									3	1		25
		2	4	5		7		9	10	11		6			8				3	1		26
		2	4	5	6			9	10	11		7			8				3	1		27
		2	4	5	6		9		10	11		7			8				3	1		28
			4	5	6	7	11	9	10						8		2		3	1		29
			4	5	6	7	11	9	10						8		2		3	1		30
		2	4	5	6	7	11	9	10	12					8*				3	1		31
		2	4	5	6	7	11	9	10	12					8*				3	1		32
		2	4	5	6	7	11	9	10						8				3	1		33
		2	4	5	6	7	11	9	10						8				3	1		34
		2	4	5	6	7	11	9	10						8	12			3	1		35
		2	4	5	6	7	11	9	10						8				3	1		36
		2	4	5	6			9	10	11					8	7			3	1		37
		2	4	5				9	10	11					8	7			3	1	6	38
		2	4	5	6	12	9		10	11					8	7			3*	1		39
		2	4	5	6		9		10	11					8	7			3	1		40
		2*	4	5	6	7			10	11					8	9		12	3	1		41
			4	5	6	9			10	11*				2	8	7		12	3	1		42
20	2	35	39	41	39	36	18	35	42	29	5	6	1	17	39	6	4	2	23	22	1	
	1	1			1	4				4	2					1		2				
		4	2	4			1	16	10	5					17		1		1			

47

1983-84

1	Aug	27	(h)	West Brom A	W	4-3	Evans, Walters, Shaw, Ormsby	29,522
2		29	(h)	Sunderland	W	1-0	Walters	20,390
3	Sep	3	(a)	QPR	L	1-2	Withe	16,922
4		7	(a)	Nottingham F	D	2-2	Withe, Shaw	16,363
5		10	(h)	Norwich C	W	1-0	Mortimer	18,887
6		17	(a)	Liverpool	L	1-2	Gibson	34,246
7		24	(h)	Southampton	W	1-0	Withe	21,209
8	Oct	1	(a)	Luton T	L	0-1		12,747
9		15	(h)	Birmingham C	W	1-0	Withe	39,318
10		23	(a)	Wolves	D	1-1	Withe	13,202
11		29	(h)	Arsenal	L	2-6	Morley, Evans (pen)	23,678
12	Nov	5	(a)	Manchester U	W	2-1	Withe 2	45,077
13		12	(h)	Stoke C	D	1-1	Withe	19,272
14		19	(h)	Leicester C	W	3-1	Withe, Rideout, McMahon	19,024
15		26	(a)	Notts Co	L	2-5	Mortimer, Evans (pen)	8,960
16	Dec	3	(h)	West Ham U	W	1-0	Rideout	21,297
17		10	(a)	Everton	D	1-1	Rideout	15,810
18		17	(h)	Ipswich T	W	4-0	Rideout, McMahon, Evans (pen), Withe	16,548
19		26	(a)	Watford	L	2-3	Curbishley, Walters	18,226
20		27	(h)	Tottenham H	D	0-0		30,125
21		31	(h)	QPR	W	2-1	Evans (pen), McMahon	19,978
22	Jan	2	(a)	Southampton	D	2-2	McMahon, Shaw	18,963
23		14	(a)	West Brom A	L	1-3	Shaw	20,399
24		20	(h)	Liverpool	L	1-3	Mortimer	19,566
25	Feb	4	(h)	Luton T	D	0-0		18,656
26		11	(a)	Norwich C	L	1-3	Shaw	14,392
27		18	(a)	Arsenal	D	1-1	Evans (pen)	26,640
28		25	(h)	Wolves	W	4-0	Withe 2, Birch, Walters	18,257
29	Mar	3	(h)	Manchester U	L	0-3		32,874
30		10	(a)	Stoke C	L	0-1		13,967
31		13	(a)	Coventry C	D	3-3	Evans (pen), Withe, Rideout	11,098
32		17	(h)	Nottingham F	W	1-0	McMahon	16,270
33		24	(a)	Sunderland	W	1-0	Walters	11,908
34		31	(a)	Birmingham C	L	1-2	Withe	23,993
35	Apr	7	(h)	Coventry C	W	2-0	Ormsby, Birch	15,318
36		14	(a)	Leicester C	L	0-2		13,366
37		18	(a)	Tottenham H	L	1-2	Walters	18,668
38		21	(h)	Watford	W	2-1	Mortimer, Foster	16,110
39		28	(h)	Notts Co	W	3-1	Walters 2, Withe	13,059
40	May	5	(a)	West Ham U	W	1-0	Mortimer	17,393
41		7	(h)	Everton	L	0-2		16,792
42		12	(a)	Ipswich T	L	1-2	Withe	20,043

FINAL LEAGUE POSITION: 10th in Division One

Appearances

Sub. Appearances

Goals

Spink	Williams	Gibson	Evans	Ormsby	Mortimer	Curbishley	Shaw	Withe	McMahon	Walters	Blair	Birch	Bremner	Day	Deacy	Dorigo	Foster	Jones	Kerr	Morley	Rideout	Walker	No.
1	2	3	4	5	6	7	8	9	10	11													1
1	2	3	4	5		7	8	9		11	6	10											2
1	2	3	4	5	6	7	8	9	10	11*											12		3
1	2	3	4	5	6	7	8*	9	10	11											12		4
1	2	3	4	5	6	7		9	10	11											8		5
1	2	3	4	5	6	7		9	10	11*										12	8		6
1	2	3	4	5	6	7		9	10	8										11			7
1	2	3	4	5	6	7	12	9		8			10							11*			8
1	2	3	4	5	6	7		9	10	8			12							11*			9
1	2	3	4	5	6			9	10*	8			7							11	12		10
1		3	4	5	6			9	10	8			7				2			11			11
1	2	3	4	5	6			9	10			8					7			11			12
	2	3*	4	5	6			9	10	12		8		1			7			11			13
1	3*		4	5	6	12		9	10	8		7					2			11			14
1	3	11	4	5	6	10		9		12		7*					2			8			15
1	2	3*	4	5	6					8		7			12					11	9	10	16
	2		4	5	6				10	11		7		1	3						9	8	17
1	2		4	5	6	7		9	10	11					3						8		18
1	2		4	5	6	7		9	10	11					3						8		19
1	2*		4	5	6	7		9	10	11					3						8	12	20
1			4	5	6	7	8	9	10	11			2		3								21
1			4	5	6		8	9	10	11		7	2									3	22
1	2	3	4		6	7	8	9	10				5								11		23
1	2	3	4		6	7	8	9	10				5								11		24
1	2	3	4		6	7	8		10	11			5								9		25
	2	11	4		6	7	8						5	1	3						9	10	26
1	2	3	4		6	7	8	9	10	11			5										27
1	2	3		4	6	7		9	10	12		8	5								11*		28
1	2	3		4	6	7*		9	10	12		8	5								11		29
1	2	3	4	5	6			9	10	8		7									11		30
1*	2	3	4	5		6		9	10	8		7								11	12		31
	2	3	4	5		6		9	10	8		7		1							11		32
	2	3	4	5		6		9	10	8		7		1							11		33
	2	3*	4	5		6		9	10	8		7	12	1							11		34
	2		4	5	6				10	11	9	8	7	1	3								35
	2		4		6				10	11	9	8	7	1	3*		5	12					36
	2	3	4		6			9	10	11	8	7		1			5						37
	2	3	4		6			9	10	11	7	8		1			5						38
	2		4		6			9	10	11	7	8		1	3		5						39
	2		4		6			9	10	11*	7	8		1	3		5				12		40
	2		4		6			9	10		7			1	3	12	5		11*		8		41
	2		4		6			9	10	11*	7	8		1	3	12	5						42
28	40	28	36	34	37	25	11	36	37	33	9	22	14	14	12		7	5	1	6	22	5	
						1	1			4		3			1	1		1	1	3	3			
		1	7	2	5	1	5	16	5	8		2					1			1	5			

49

1984-85

1	Aug	25	(h)	Coventry C	W	1-0	Bremner	20,970
2		27	(a)	Stoke C	W	3-1	Walters 2, Withe	12,605
3	Sep	1	(a)	Newcastle U	L	0-3		31,497
4		5	(h)	Nottingham F	L	0-5		17,730
5		8	(h)	Chealsea	W	4-2	Foster, Rideout, Withe 2	21,494
6		15	(a)	Watford	D	3-3	Foster, McMahon, Withe	16,440
7		22	(h)	Tottenham H	L	0-1		22,409
8		29	(a)	Ipswich T	L	0-3		15,630
9	Oct	6	(h)	Manchester U	W	3-0	Evans, Rideout, Withe	37,132
10		13	(a)	Everton	L	1-2	Withe	25,089
11		20	(h)	Norwich C	D	2-2	Withe 2	14,149
12		27	(a)	Leicester C	L	0-5		11,885
13	Nov	3	(h)	West Ham U	D	0-0		15,709
14		10	(a)	Arsenal	D	1-1	Birch	33,195
15		17	(h)	Southampton	D	2-2	Six, Withe	13,937
16		24	(a)	QPR	L	0-2		11,689
17	Dec	1	(h)	Sunderland	W	1-0	Rideout	14,669
18		8	(a)	Luton T	L	0-1		7,696
19		15	(h)	Liverpool	D	0-0		24,007
20		22	(h)	Newcastle U	W	4-0	Evans (pen), Rideout 3	14,491
21		26	(a)	Sheffield W	D	1-1	Rideout	30,971
22		29	(a)	Nottingham F	L	2-3	Gibson, Rideout	17,676
23	Jan	1	(h)	West Brom A	W	3-1	Birch, Gibson, Rideout	31,710
24		19	(a)	Coventry C	W	3-0	Rideout, Walters 2	15,226
25	Feb	2	(h)	Ipswich T	W	2-1	Cowans, Gibson	15,051
26		23	(a)	West Ham U	W	2-1	Ormsby, Walters	14,845
27	Mar	2	(h)	Leicester C	L	0-1		16,285
28		9	(a)	Norwich C	D	2-2	Evans 2 (2 pens)	21,853
29		13	(h)	Arsenal	D	0-0		15,487
30		16	(h)	Everton	D	1-1	Evans (pen)	22,625
31		23	(a)	Manchester U	L	0-4		40,941
32		27	(h)	Stoke C	W	2-0	Berry (og), Six	10,874
33		30	(a)	Tottenham H	W	2-0	Rideout, Walters	27,971
34	Apr	6	(h)	Sheffield W	W	3-0	Evans (pen), Ormsby, Rideout	18,308
35		8	(a)	West Brom A	L	0-1		21,044
36		16	(a)	Chelsea	L	1-3	Walters	13,267
37		20	(a)	Southampton	L	0-2		15,736
38		24	(h)	Watford	D	1-1	Walters	11,493
39		27	(h)	QPR	W	5-2	Rideout 2, Walters, Withe 2	12,023
40	May	4	(a)	Sunderland	W	4-0	Gibson, McMahon, Walters, Withe	12,467
41		6	(h)	Luton T	L	0-1		14,130
42		11	(a)	Liverpool	L	1-2	Birch	33,001

FINAL LEAGUE POSITION: 10th in Division One

Appearances

Sub. Appearances

Goals

Day	Williams	Gibson	Evans	Foster	McMahon	Bremner	Walters	Withe	Cowans	Mortimer	Birch	Bradley	Curbishley	Dorigo	Daley	Glover	Kerr	Norton	Ormsby	Poole	Rideout	Spink	Six	Walker	
1	2	3	4	5	6	7	8	9	10	11															1
1	2	3	4	5	6	7	8	9	10	11															2
1	2	3	4	5	6	7	8	9	10	11															3
1	2	3	4	5	6	7	8	9	10	11*											12				4
1		2	4	5	6		11	9	10		7			3							8				5
1		2	4	5	6		11	9	10		7			3							8				6
1	9	2	4	5	6		11		10		7			3							8				7
1	2	3	4				11*	9	10	6	7						12		5		8				8
1	2	3	4		6		12	9	10		7								5		8		11*		9
1	2		4		6			9	10		7			3			12		5		8		11		10
1	2	3	4		6*			9	10	12	7								5		8		11		11
1	2	3	4		6			9	10		7						12		5		8*		11		12
1	2	3	4		6			9	10		7								5				11		13
1	2	3	4		6			9	10		7			12			8		5				11*		14
1	2	3	4		6			9	10		7			12			8*		5				11		15
1	2	3	4		6		8	9	10		7								5				11		16
	2*	3	4		6		11	9	10				7	12					5		8	1			17
	2	3	4		6*		11	9	10				7	12					5		8	1			18
	2	10	4				11	9			7		6	3					5		8	1			19
	2	10	4		6*		11	9			7			3					5		8	1		12	20
	2	10	4		6		11	9			7			3					5		8*	1		12	21
	2	10	4		6		11	9			7			3					5		8	1			22
	2	10	4*		6		11	9	12		7			3					5		8	1			23
		10			6		11	9			7			3	4			2	5		8	1			24
		7	4		6		11	9	10					3				2	5		8	1			25
	2	6	4				11	9	10		7			3					5		8	1			26
	2	6	4		12		11	9	10		7			3					5		8*	1			27
	2	7	4		6*		11	9	10					3		8			5			1			28
	2	7	4		6		11	9	10					3		8			5			1		6	29
	2		4		6		11	9	10					3		8			5			1	12	7*	30
	2	7	4		6		11	9	10					3					5			1	8		31
	2	10	4*		6		11	9						3					5		8	1	7	12	32
	2	10			6		11	9						3*	4				5	1	8		7	12	33
	2	3	4		6		11	9	10										5	1	8		7		34
	2	10	4		6		11	9						3					5	1	8		7*	12	35
	2	10	4		6		11	9			7			3					5		8	1			36
	2	10	4		6		11				7			3	8				5		9	1		6	37
	2	10	4		6		11	9			7			3	7				5		8	1		6	38
	2	7	4		6		11	9	10					3	6				5	1	8				39
	2	8			6		11*	9	10		7	4		3		5	12					1			40
	2	8	4		6		11*	9	10		7			3		5	12					1			41
	2	10	4		6		11	9	12					3	7*				5	1	8				42
16	38	41	38	8	34	4	35	40	29	5	24	1	3	27	4	5	6	2	32	7	28	19	13	4	
					1		1			1	1	1	1			4	1		4		1		3	3	
		4	6	2	2	1	10	12	1		3								2		14		2		

51

1985-86

1	Aug	17	(a)	Manchester U	L	0-4		49,743
2		21	(h)	Liverpool	D	2-2	Shaw, Walters	20,197
3		24	(h)	QPR	L	1-2	Walters	11,896
4		27	(a)	Southampton	D	0-0		14,220
5		31	(h)	Luton T	W	3-1	Walters, Hodge, Norton	10,524
6	Sep	4	(a)	West Brom A	W	3-0	Evans (pen), Daley, Walters	17,077
7		7	(a)	Birmingham C	D	0-0		24,971
8		14	(h)	Coventry C	D	1-1	Hodge	12,198
9		21	(a)	Ipswich T	W	3-0	Walters, Hodge, Birch	11,598
10		28	(h)	Everton	D	0-0		22,048
11	Oct	5	(a)	Arsenal	L	2-3	Stainrod, Walters	18,881
12		12	(h)	Nottingham F	L	1-2	Gibson	15,315
13		19	(a)	West Ham U	L	1-4	Stainrod	15,034
14		26	(h)	Newcastle U	L	1-2	Gray	12,633
15	Nov	2	(h)	Oxford U	W	2-0	Evans (pen), Stainrod	12,922
16		9	(a)	Watford	D	1-1	Gray	14,085
17		16	(h)	Sheffield W	D	1-1	Gibson	13,849
18		23	(a)	Chelsea	L	1-2	Gray	17,509
19		30	(h)	Tottenham H	L	1-2	Walters	14,099
20	Dec	7	(a)	Liverpool	L	0-3		29,418
21		14	(h)	Manchester U	L	1-3	Hodge	27,626
22		17	(a)	QPR	W	1-0	Birch	11,237
23		26	(a)	Leicester C	L	1-3	Walters	13,752
24		28	(h)	West Brom A	D	1-1	Kerr	18,796
25	Jan	1	(h)	Manchester C	L	0-1		14,215
26		11	(a)	Coventry C	D	3-3	Stainrod, Gray, Elliott	10,328
27		18	(a)	Luton T	L	0-2		10,217
28	Feb	1	(h)	Southampton	D	0-0		8,456
29	Mar	1	(a)	Everton	L	0-2		32,133
30		8	(h)	Arsenal	L	1-4	Walters	10,584
31		15	(a)	Nottingham F	D	1-1	Walters	12,933
32		19	(h)	West Ham U	W	2-1	Hodge 2	11,567
33		22	(h)	Birmingham C	L	0-3		26,694
34		29	(a)	Manchester C	D	2-2	Hodge, Stainrod	20,935
35		31	(h)	Leicester C	W	1-0	Stainrod	12,200
36	Apr	5	(a)	Oxford U	D	1-1	Stainrod	11,406
37		9	(a)	Newcastle U	D	2-2	Daley, Hunt	20,107
38		12	(h)	Watford	W	4-1	Dorigo, Evans (pen), Gray, Stainrod	12,781
39		16	(h)	Ipswich T	W	1-0	Hodge	13,611
40		19	(a)	Sheffield W	L	0-2		19,782
41		26	(h)	Chelsea	W	3-1	Norton, Hunt, Stainrod	17,770
42	May	3	(a)	Tottenham H	L	2-4	Stainrod, Elliott	14,854

FINAL LEAGUE POSITION: 16th in Division One

Appearances

Sub. Appearances

Goals

Spink	Williams	Dorigo	Evans	Ormsby	McMahon	Birch	Shaw	Gray	Gibson	Walters	Bradley	Daley	Glover	Walker	Norton	Hodge	Stainrod	Elliott	Poole	Kerr	Hunt	Blair	#
1	2	3	4	5	6	7	8	9	10*	11	12												1
1	2	3		5	6	7	8	9		11		12	4	10									2
1		3		5	6	7	8	9		11		12	4	10*	2								3
1		3		5		7		9*		8	6	11	4	12	2	10							4
1		3		5		7				11	6	8	4	9	2	10							5
1	2	3	4	5		7		9		11	6	8				10							6
1	2	3	4	5		7		9		8	6*	11	12			10							7
1	2	3	4	5		7		9	6	8		11				10							8
1	2	3	4	5		7		9*	6	8	12	11				10							9
1	2	3	4	5		7		9		11	6					10	8						10
1	2	3	4	5		7		9		11	6					10	8						11
1	2	3	4	5		7*		9	6	11		12				10	8						12
1	2*	3	4	5		7		9		11	12		6			10	8						13
1		3	4	5*		7		9		11		12		6	2	10	8						14
1	2	3	4					9	6	11		7	5			10	8						15
1	2	3	4					9	6	11		7	5			10	8						16
1	2	3	4					9	6	11		7	5			10	8						17
1	2	3	4			12		9		11	6	7*	5			10	8						18
1		3	4			7	9*			11	6	12	5		2	10	8						19
1	2	3					12	9		11	6	7	4			10	8*	5					20
1	2	3	4					9		11	6	7				10	8	5					21
	2	3				7		9		11	6		4			10	8	5	1				22
	2	3				7	8			11	6*	12	4			10	9	5	1				23
1		3	4			6				11		7			2	10	9	5		8			24
1		3	4			6		9		11		7*			2	10	8	5		12			25
1		3	4			6		9		11					2	10	8	5		7			26
1	3		4			6	12	9		11			10		2		8*	5		7			27
		3	4				8	9			7*		6		2	10	12	5	1	11			28
1		3*	4			7				11	6	12			2	10	9	5		8			29
1			4			7		9		11	6	3			2	10	8	5					30
1	2	3	4			12	8*	9		11						10		5			6	7	31
1	2	3	4				8	9		11						10		5			6	7	32
1	2	3	4				8	9		11						10		5			6	7	33
	2*	3	4					9				11	12			10	8	5	1		6	7	34
		3	4					9		11					2	10	8	5	1		6	7	35
		3	4					9		11					2	10	8	5	1		6	7	36
		3	4							11		9			2	10	8	5	1		6	7	37
		3	4					9		11					2	10	8	5	1		6	7	38
		3	4					9		11*	12				2	10	8	5	1		6	7	39
1		3	4					9*		11	12				2	10	8	5			6	7	40
	3		4			10		9		11					2		8	5	1		6	7	41
	3		4			10	9			11					2		8	5	1		6	7	42
31	25	38	35	14	3	25	10	35	7	40	15	16	15	5	20	36	29	23	11	5	12	12	
						2	2			3	7	3	2				1			1			
		1	3			2	1	5	2	10		2			2	8	10	2		1	2		

1986-87

1	Aug	23	(h)	Tottenham H	L	0-3		24,712
2		26	(a)	Wimbledon	L	2-3	Evans (pen), Thompson	6,366
3		30	(a)	QPR	L	0-1		13,003
4	Sep	3	(h)	Luton T	W	2-1	Kerr 2	13,122
5		6	(h)	Oxford U	L	1-2	Stainrod (pen)	14,668
6		13	(a)	Nottingham F	L	0-6		17,045
7		20	(h)	Norwich C	L	1-4	Stainrod	12,304
8		27	(a)	Liverpool	D	3-3	Hodge, Thompson, Evans (pen)	38,298
9	Oct	4	(a)	Coventry C	W	1-0	Thompson	18,563
10		11	(h)	Southampton	W	3-1	Elliott 2, Evans (pen)	16,211
11		18	(a)	Watford	L	2-4	Walters, Stainrod	16,414
12		25	(h)	Newcastle U	W	2-0	Hodge 2	16,614
13	Nov	1	(h)	Leicester C	W	2-0	Stainrod 2	14,529
14		8	(a)	Manchester C	L	1-3	Daley	22,875
15		15	(h)	Chelsea	D	0-0		17,739
16		22	(a)	West Ham U	D	1-1	Thompson	21,959
17		29	(h)	Arsenal	L	0-4		21,658
18	Dec	6	(a)	Sheffield W	L	1-2	Evans (pen)	21,144
19		13	(h)	Manchester U	D	3-3	Hodge, Thompson, Evans (pen)	29,205
20		20	(a)	Oxford U	D	2-2	Thompson, Walters	8,364
21		26	(h)	Charlton A	W	2-0	Birch, Daley	16,692
22		27	(a)	Chelsea	L	1-4	Elliott	14,637
23	Jan	1	(a)	Everton	L	0-3		40,203
24		3	(h)	Nottingham F	D	0-0		19,159
25		24	(a)	Tottenham H	L	0-3		19,121
26	Feb	7	(h)	QPR	L	0-1		13,109
27		14	(a)	Luton T	L	1-2	Evans (pen)	9,174
28		21	(h)	Liverpool	D	2-2	Lawrenson (og), Elliott	32,093
29		28	(a)	Norwich C	D	1-1	Elliott	15,070
30	Mar	4	(h)	Wimbledon	D	0-0		12,484
31		7	(a)	Newcastle U	L	1-2	Daley	21,224
32		21	(a)	Southampton	L	0-5		13,686
33		25	(h)	Watford	D	1-1	Hunt	12,575
34		28	(h)	Coventry C	W	1-0	Birch	18,689
35	Apr	4	(h)	Manchester C	D	0-0		18,241
36		11	(a)	Leicester C	D	1-1	Walters	11,933
37		18	(h)	Everton	L	0-1		31,218
38		20	(a)	Charlton A	L	0-3		5,595
39		25	(h)	West Ham U	W	4-0	Hunt, Aspinall 2, Stainrod	13,584
40	May	2	(a)	Arsenal	L	1-2	Aspinall	18,463
41		4	(h)	Sheffield W	L	1-2	Robinson	15,007
42		9	(a)	Manchester U	L	1-3	Birch	35,179

FINAL LEAGUE POSITION: 22nd in Division One

Appearances

Sub. Appearances

Goals

Poole	Williams	Dorigo	Evans	Elliott	Blair	Hunt	Stainrod	Thompson	Hodge	Daley	Keown	Birch	Kerr	Norton	Spink	Gray	Walters	Shaw	Glover	Cooper	Aspinall	Robinson	Burke	Gallacher	Ritchie	No.
1	2	3	4	5	6	7	8	9	10	11																1
1	2	3	4	5	6	7	8	9	10	11																2
1		3	4	5	6	7*	8		10	11	2	12	9													3
1		3	4	5	6*	7	8	9	10	11	2		12													4
1		3	4*	5		7	8	9	10	11	2	12	6													5
1		3	4	5		7	8	9		11	2	6		10												6
1		3	4	5		6	8	9	10	11	2	7														7
		3	4	5		11	8	9	10		6	7		2	1											8
		3	4	5		11	8*	9	10		6	7		2	1	12										9
		3	4	5		6	8		10			7	12	2	1	9*	11									10
		3	4	5		8	12	9			6*	7		2	1		11									11
		3	4			6		9	10	8	5	7		2	1		11									12
	2	3	4			6	8	9	10	11	5			7	1											13
		3	4	12		6	8*		10	11	5	7		2	1	9										14
	2	3	4	5		10	12	9		11	5			7	1			8*								15
	2	3	4	5		10*		9	11	12	6		8	7	1											16
	2	3	4	5			9		10	11	6		8*	7	1		12									17
		3	4			7	6	8	10	11			2	1	9*	12		5								18
		3	4			7	6	8	10	11			2	1	9			5								19
	2	3		5		6	8		7	4				10	1	9	11									20
	2	3		5		6	8		7	4	12			10*	1	9	11									21
	2	3		5		10	6	8	12	4	7*				1	9	11									22
		3	4	5		10	6	8	11	12	7*			2	1	9										23
	2	3	4			10	9	8	7	5			12		1		11			6*						24
	2	3	4			10		8	12	5	7				1	9	11			6*						25
	2	3	4			10	9*	8	12	5	7				1		11			6						26
	2	3	4	5		10		9	8	6	7				1		11									27
	2	3		5		10		9	12	4	7				1	11*				6	8					28
		3		5		10		9	11	4				2	1				6	7	8					29
		3	11	5		10		9	7	4				2	1					6	8					30
		3	11	5		10	12	9	7	4				2*	1					6	8					31
		3	4	5		10	9			2	7				1		11				8	6				32
	2	3		5		10	8		12	4	7*				1	9	11			6						33
	2	3		5		10	8*	12		4	7				1	9	11			6						34
	2	3		5		10*	12	8		4	7				1	9	11			6						35
	2	3		5		10			12	4	7				1	9	11			6*	8					36
	2	3	12	5		10				4	7				1	9				6	8	11*				37
	2	3		5		10			11	4	7				1	9				6	8					38
1	2	3		5		10	6		11*	4	7					9	12				8					39
1	2	3		5		10	6		12	4	7*					9	11				8					40
1	2	3		5*		10			11	4	7					9				6	8	12				41
	2					6	8			4	7				1	9*			5	10	11		3	12		42
10	26	41	25	33	4	39	25	30	17	25	35	26	4	19	32	18	18	1	5	13	12	2	1	1		
			1	1			4	1		8	1	3	2	1		1	3				1		1			
			6	5		2	6	6	4	3			3	2			3				3	1				

55

1987-88

#	Month	Date		Opponent		Result	Scorers	Attendance
1	Aug	15	(a)	Ipswich T	D	1-1	O'Donnell (og)	14,580
2		22	(h)	Birmingham C	L	0-2		30,870
3		29	(a)	Hull C	L	1-2	Aspinall (pen)	8,315
4		31	(h)	Manchester C	D	1-1	Gage	16,282
5	Sep	5	(a)	Leicester C	W	2-0	Walters, Lillis	10,286
6		8	(h)	Middlesbrough	L	0-1		12,665
7		12	(h)	Barnsley	D	0-0		12,621
8		16	(a)	West Brom A	W	2-0	Aspinall 2	22,072
9		19	(a)	Huddersfield T	W	1-0	Hunt S	6,884
10		26	(h)	Sheffield U	D	1-1	Gage	14,761
11		30	(h)	Blackburn R	D	1-1	Aspinall	11,772
12	Oct	3	(a)	Plymouth A	W	3-1	Walters 2, Lillis	10,515
13		10	(a)	Leeds U	W	3-1	Rennie (og), Aspinall 2	20,741
14		17	(h)	Bournemouth	D	1-1	Walters	15,145
15		21	(h)	Crystal Palace	W	4-1	Walters 3 (1 pen), Hunt S	12,755
16		24	(a)	Stoke C	D	0-0		13,494
17		31	(h)	Reading	W	2-1	Blair, Lillis	13,413
18	Nov	3	(a)	Shrewsbury T	W	2-1	Keown, Aspinall	7,089
19		7	(h)	Millwall	L	1-2	Keown	13,255
20		14	(a)	Oldham A	W	1-0	McInally	6,469
21		28	(a)	Bradford C	W	4-2	Gray S 2, Birch, Thompson	15,006
22	Dec	5	(h)	Swindon T	W	2-1	Thompson 2	16,127
23		12	(a)	Birmingham C	W	2-1	Thompson 2	27,759
24		18	(h)	West Brom A	D	0-0		24,437
25		26	(a)	Sheffield U	D	1-1	Thompson	15,809
26		28	(h)	Huddersfield T	D	1-1	Birch	20,948
27	Jan	1	(h)	Hull C	W	5-0	Gray S, Aspinall 2, Gray A, McInally	19,236
28		2	(a)	Barnsley	W	3-1	Aspinall, Birch, McInally	11,562
29		16	(h)	Ipswich T	W	1-0	Keown	20,201
30		23	(a)	Manchester C	W	2-0	Daley, Thompson	24,668
31	Feb	6	(h)	Leicester C	W	2-1	Lillis, Evans	18,867
32		14	(a)	Middlesbrough	L	1-2	Daley	16,957
33		20	(a)	Blackburn R	L	2-3	Platt, Hendry (og)	17,356
34		27	(h)	Plymouth A	W	5-2	Gray S (pen), Platt, Birch 2, Thompson	16,142
35	Mar	5	(a)	Bournemouth	W	2-1	Daley, Platt	10,057
36		12	(h)	Leeds U	L	1-2	McInally	19,677
37		19	(a)	Reading	W	2-0	Birch, Thompson	10,033
38		26	(h)	Stoke C	L	0-1		20,392
39	Apr	2	(a)	Millwall	L	1-2	Thompson	13,697
40		4	(h)	Oldham A	L	1-2	Gray S	19,138
41		9	(a)	Crystal Palace	D	1-1	Platt	16,476
42		23	(h)	Shrewsbury T	W	1-0	Aspinall	18,396
43	May	2	(h)	Bradford C	W	1-0	Platt	36,423
44		7	(a)	Swindon T	D	0-0		10,959

FINAL LEAGUE POSITION: 2nd in Division Two

Appearances

Sub. Appearances

Goals

Spink	Gage	Gallacher	Cooper	Sims	Keown	Birch	Aspinall	Stainrod	Hunt D	Walters	Hunt S	Daley	Burke	Allen	Lillis	McNally	Evans	Shaw	Blair	Gray A	Thompson	Gray S	Norton	Platt	Williams	No.
1	2	3	4	5	6	7	8	9	10	11																1
1	2	3	4	5	6	7	8	9†	10*	11	12	14														2
1	2	3	4	5	6		8	9	10	11		7*	12													3
1	2	3		5	6		8	9	4	11	10	7														4
1	2	3		5	6				4	11	10	7	8	9												5
1	2	3	14	5	6		12		4†	11	10	7*	8	9												6
1	2	3	4	5	6	7	12			11	10		8*	9												7
1	2	3	4	5	6	7	8			11	10			9												8
1	2	3	4*	5	6	7	8		12	11	10					9										9
1	2	3		5	6	7	8		4	11		12	10*			9										10
1	2	3		5	6	7	8		10						4	9*	12									11
1	2	3		5	6	7	8			11	10				4	9*	12									12
1	2	3		5	6	7	8			11	10				4	9										13
1	2	3		5	6	7	8*			11	10				4			12								14
1	2	3		5	6	7	8		9	11	10				4											15
1	2	3		5	6	7	8*		10	11					4	9	12									16
1	2	3		5	6	7	8		10*	11					4	9	12									17
1	2	3		5	6	7	8			11					4	9			10							18
1	2	3		5	6	7	8			11					4	9	12		10*							19
1	2	3		5	6	7	8			11					4	9			10							20
1	2	3		5	6	11	8									7				4	9	10				21
1	2	3		5	6	7	8			11						7				4	9	10				22
1	2	3		5	6	7	8			11					4						9	10				23
1	2	3		5	6	7	8*			11					4	12					9	10				24
1	2	3		5	6	7	8*			11					4	12					9	10				25
1	2	3		5	6	7	8*			11						12				4	9	10				26
1	2	3			6	7	12								8	11	5			4	9	10*				27
1	2	3			6	7	10*								8	11	5			4	9		12			28
1	2	3			6	7									8	11	5		10	4	9					29
1	2	3			6	7					10				8	11	5			4	9					30
1	2	3			6	7					10				8	11	5			4	9					31
1	2	3			6	7					10*				8	11	5			4	9	12				32
1	2	3			6	7*					12				8		5			4	9	10		11		33
1	2	3			6	7					8						5			4	9	10		11		34
1	2	3			6	7					8						5			4	9	10		11		35
1	2	3			6	7*					8					12	5			4	9	10		11		36
1	2	3			6	7					8*					12	5			4	9	10		11		37
1	2	3			6	7					12			14	8†		5			4	9*	10		11		38
1	2	3			6	7*	8†				12			4	14		5				9	10		11		39
1	2		3		6	7†	12				8*				14		5				9	10	4	11		40
1	2	3			6	7									12		5				9	10		8	11*	41
1	2	3			6		11				7			8			5			4	9	10				42
1	2	3	6				8								7		5			4	9	10		11		43
1	2	3		5		7	8										6			4	9	10		11		44
44	44	43	6	29	42	38	28	4	11	24	10	10	4	4	28	18	18	1	3	19	24	19	1	11	1	
		1				4		1		1		4	2		1	8	2	3	1			1	1			
	2			3	6	11			7	2	3				4	4	1		1	1	11	5		5		

1988-89

1	Aug	27	(h)	Millwall	D	2-2	Gray S (pen), McInally	22,449
2	Sep	3	(a)	Arsenal	W	3-2	McInally 2, Gray A	37,413
3		10	(h)	Liverpool	D	1-1	McInally	41,409
4		17	(a)	West Ham U	D	2-2	McInally 2	19,186
5		24	(h)	Nottingham F	D	1-1	Gage	23,029
6	Oct	1	(a)	Sheffield W	L	0-1		18,301
7		8	(h)	Wimbledon	L	0-1		15,416
8		15	(a)	Charlton A	D	2-2	McInally, Platt	7,594
9		22	(h)	Everton	W	2-0	Daley, Platt	26,636
10		29	(h)	Tottenham H	W	2-1	Fenwick (og), Daley	26,238
11	Nov	5	(a)	Manchester U	D	1-1	Cowans	44,804
12		12	(a)	Southampton	L	1-3	Daley	16,007
13		19	(h)	Derby Co	L	1-2	Mountfield	23,489
14		26	(a)	Coventry C	L	1-2	McInally	20,104
15	Dec	3	(h)	Norwich C	W	3-1	Gage 2, Platt	19,653
16		10	(a)	Middlesbrough	D	3-3	Gray A, McInally 2	18,096
17		17	(a)	Luton T	D	1-1	Johnson M (og)	8,785
18		26	(h)	QPR	W	2-1	McInally 2	25,106
19		31	(h)	Arsenal	L	0-3		32,486
20	Jan	3	(a)	Liverpool	L	0-1		39,014
21		14	(h)	Newcastle U	W	3-1	Gray A, Daley, McInally	21,010
22		21	(a)	Nottingham F	L	0-4		22,662
23	Feb	4	(h)	Sheffield W	W	2-0	Callaghan, Platt	19,334
24		11	(a)	Wimbledon	L	0-1		6,201
25		14	(a)	Everton	D	1-1	Ormondroyd	20,142
26		25	(h)	Charlton A	L	1-2	Cowans	16,481
27	Mar	1	(a)	Tottenham H	L	0-2		19,090
28		12	(h)	Manchester U	D	0-0		28,332
29		18	(a)	Millwall	L	0-2		13,206
30		25	(h)	West Ham U	L	0-1		22,471
31		27	(a)	QPR	L	0-1		11,378
32	Apr	1	(h)	Luton T	W	2-1	Daley, Olney	15,640
33		8	(a)	Newcastle U	W	2-1	Gray S, Platt	20,329
34		22	(a)	Norwich C	D	2-2	Olney, McInally	14,550
35		29	(h)	Middlesbrough	D	1-1	Gray S	18,950
36	May	2	(h)	Southampton	L	1-2	Gray S	15,218
37		6	(a)	Derby Co	L	1-2	Platt	18,112
38		13	(h)	Coventry C	D	1-1	Platt	29,906

FINAL LEAGUE POSITION: 17th in Division One

Appearances

Sub. Appearances

Goals

Spink	Price	Gage	Gray A	Evans	Keown	Birch	Platt	McInally	Cowans	Gray S	Daley	Thompson	Sims	Mountfield	Gallacher	Olney	Callaghan	Ormondroyd	Butler	Williams	Lillis	Duffy	Hunt	No.
1	2	3	4†	5	6	7*	8	9	10	11	12	14												1
1	2		4	5	6		8	9	10	11	7		3											2
1	2	3	4	5	6	12	8	9†	10	11	7*	14												3
1	2	12	4	5*	6		8	9	10	11	7			3										4
1	2	3	4		6		8	9*	10	11†	7	12		6	14									5
1	2	5	4		6		8		10	11	7	9		3										6
1	2	5	4	12	6		8		10	11	7	9*		3										7
1	2	5		4	6		8	12	10	11	7			3		9*								8
1	2	5		4	6		8	9	10	11	7			3										9
1	2	3		4	6		8	9	10	11	7			3										10
1	2	5		4	6		8	9	10		7			3	11									11
1	2	5	12	4	6		8	9	10		7*			3	11									12
1	2	5	12	4	6		8	9	10		7			3	11*									13
1	2	4	7		6	12	8	9	10	3	11*			5										14
1	2	4	7	5	6		8	9	10	3	11													15
1	2	4*	7	5	6	12†	8	9	10	3	11			14										16
1	2	4	7	5	6	12	8	9	10	3	11*													17
1	2	4	7	5			8	9	10	3	11				6									18
1	2	4	7*	5	12		8	9	10	3	11				6									19
1	2	4	12	5	6		8	9†	10*	11	7			3		14								20
1	2*	4	7		6		8	9	10	3	11			5		12								21
1		2	4*		6	7	8	9	10	3	12			5		11								22
1	2	4			6		8	9	10	3				5		7	11							23
1	2	4			6	12	8	9	10*	3				5		7	11							24
	2	4			6		8	9	10	3				5		7	11		1					25
1	2	4	6*	12			8		10	3	9*			5		7	11							26
1	2	4			6	7	8		10	3				5			11	9						27
	2	4			6	7	8	9		3			5			12	11	10*	1					28
	2	4†			6	7*	8	9	14	3			5			12	11	10	1					29
	2				6	4		9*	10†	3	8		5	14		12	7		1	11				30
1	2		4*		6		7		10	14			5	3		9	12	11			8†			31
1	2	4			6		8	9	10	3	11*			5		12	7							32
1	2	4			6		8	9	10	3				5		11	7							33
1	2	4			6		8	9	10*	3				5		11	7	12						34
1	2	4			6		8	9		3	10*			5		11	7	12						35
1	2	4			6		8	9*		3	12			5		11	7	10						36
1					14		8	9		3	10*			5		11	7†	12			4	2	6	37
1	2	4			6	7	8	9*	10	3				5		12	11							38
34	36	27	15	26	32	6	38	32	32	35	25	2	12	22	3	8	15	9	4	1	2	1	1	
	1		3	1	2	6		1	1		4	3		2	1	7	1	3						
		3	3				7	14	2	4	5			1		2	1	1						

1989-90

#	Month	Date		Opponent		Score	Scorers	Attendance
1	Aug	19	(a)	Nottingham F	D	1-1	Mountfield	26,766
2		23	(h)	Liverpool	D	1-1	Platt	35,796
3		26	(h)	Charlton A	D	1-1	Olney	15,236
4		29	(h)	Southampton	L	1-2	Platt	14,401
5	Sep	9	(h)	Tottenham H	W	2-0	Olney 2	24,769
6		16	(a)	Sheffield W	L	0-1		17,509
7		23	(h)	QPR	L	1-3	Platt	14,170
8		30	(h)	Derby Co	W	1-0	Platt	16,245
9	Oct	14	(a)	Luton T	W	1-0	Mountfield	9,433
10		22	(a)	Manchester C	W	2-0	Daley, Olney	23,354
11		28	(h)	Crystal Palace	W	2-1	Platt 2	15,724
12	Nov	5	(a)	Everton	W	6-2	Cowans, Olney 2, Platt 2, Nielsen	17,637
13		11	(a)	Norwich C	L	0-2		18,186
14		18	(h)	Coventry C	W	4-1	Ormondroyd 2, Peake (og), Platt (pen)	22,803
15		25	(a)	Wimbledon	W	2-0	Platt, Daley	5,888
16	Dec	2	(h)	Nottingham F	W	2-1	Olney, Platt	25,575
17		9	(a)	Liverpool	D	1-1	Olney	37,435
18		16	(a)	Millwall	L	0-2		10,528
19		26	(h)	Manchester U	W	3-0	Olney, Platt, Gage	41,247
20		30	(h)	Arsenal	W	2-1	Platt, Mountfield	40,665
21	Jan	1	(a)	Chelsea	W	3-0	Gage, Daley, Platt	23,990
22		13	(a)	Charlton A	W	2-0	Mountfield, McLaughlin (og)	10,513
23		20	(h)	Southampton	W	2-1	Daley, Gage	33,118
24	Feb	10	(h)	Sheffield W	W	1-0	Platt	27,168
25		21	(a)	Tottenham H	W	2-0	Ormondroyd, Platt	32,472
26		24	(h)	Wimbledon	L	0-3		29,325
27	Mar	4	(a)	Coventry C	L	0-2		17,891
28		10	(h)	Luton T	W	2-0	Daley, Platt	22,505
29		17	(a)	Derby Co	W	1-0	Ormondroyd	21,062
30		20	(a)	QPR	D	1-1	Nielsen	15,856
31		24	(a)	Crystal Palace	L	0-1		18,586
32	Apr	1	(h)	Manchester C	L	1-2	Cowans	24,797
33		11	(a)	Arsenal	W	1-0	Price	30,060
34		14	(h)	Chelsea	W	1-0	Cowans	28,361
35		17	(a)	Manchester U	L	0-2		44,080
36		21	(h)	Millwall	W	1-0	Platt	21,028
37		28	(h)	Norwich C	D	3-3	McGrath, Cascarino, Platt	28,988
38	May	5	(a)	Everton	D	3-3	Cascarino, Cowans, Daley	29,551

FINAL LEAGUE POSITION: 2nd in Division One

Appearances

Sub. Appearances

Goals

Spink	Price	Gray	McGrath	Mountfield	Nielsen	Birch	Heath	Platt	Cowans	Daley	Olney	Callaghan	Comyn	Williams	Gallacher	Ormondroyd	Gage	Blake	Cascarino	Yorke	
1	2	3	4	5	6	7	8	9	10*	11†	12	14									1
1		3	4	5	6	7	8†	9	10		12	11*	2	14							2
1	2	3	4	5	6*	7	8	9	10	11†	12				14						3
1	2	10	4	5	6*	7	8	9			12	11†				3	14				4
1	2	10	6	5			8	7			9	11				3		4			5
1	2	10	6	5	12		8*	7			9†	11				3	14	4			6
1	2	10	6	5	12		8	7			9	11†				3	14	4*			7
1	2	11	6	5				8	10	7	9*					3	12	4			8
1	2	11		5	6	14	8†	4	10	12	9			3*				7			9
1	2	11		5	6	12		8	10	7	9					3		4*			10
1	2	11		5	6	12		8	10	7	9†					3	14	4*			11
1	2		4	5	6	12		8	10	7	9*					11	3†	14			12
1	2	4†	5	6				8	10		9	7	3	12		11*		14			13
1	2	3	4	5	6			8	10	7	9*			12		11					14
1	2	3	4	5	6			8	10	7	9					11					15
1	2	3	4	5	6			8	10	7	9					11					16
1	2	3	4	5	6			8	10	7	9					11					17
1	2	3†	4	5	6*			8	10	7	9			12		11		14			18
1			4	5	6	12		8	10	7*	9					11	3	2			19
1			4	5	6			8	10	7	9					11	3	2			20
1	12		4	5	6*			8	10	7	9					11	3	2			21
1	2		4	5	6			8	10	7	9					11	3				22
1	2		4	5	6			8	10	7	9					11	3				23
1	2		4	5	6			8	10	7	9					11	3				24
1	2		4	5	6			8	10	7	9					11	3				25
1	2	14	4	5	6	12		8	10	7	9*					11†	3				26
1	2	14	4	5†	6	12		8	10	7	9					11*	3				27
1	2	5	4		6			8	10	7	9			11			3				28
1	2	5	4		6			8	10	7		11*				12	3		9		29
1	2*	5	4		6			8	10	7	12					11	3		9		30
1	2	5	4		6			8	10	7†	12					11*	3		9	14	31
1		5	4		6			8	10	7	2					11*	3		9	12	32
1	2	12	4		6	11		8	10	7			5			3*			9		33
1	2	3	4	5*	6	11		8	10	7			12						9		34
1	2	3	4	5*	6			8	10	7			12			11			9		35
1	2	3	4	5*	6			8	10	7			12		14	11†			9		36
1	2	3	4	5	6			8	10	7	9					11					37
1	2*	3	4	5	6				10	7	9			12		11	8				38
38	33	26	35	32	34	6	8	37	34	31	27	7	3	4	6	19	22	6	10		
	1	3			2	6	1			1	8	1	1	6	1	6		3	2		
	1		1	4	2			19	4	6	9					4	3		2		

1990-91

1	Aug	25	(h)	Southampton	D 1-1	Cascarino	29,542
2	Sep	1	(a)	Liverpool	L 1-2	Platt	38,061
3		5	(a)	Manchester C	L 1-2	Platt (pen)	30,199
4		8	(h)	Coventry C	W 2-1	Platt (pen), Cascarino	27,001
5		15	(a)	Derby Co	W 2-0	Daley, Platt	19,024
6		22	(h)	QPR	D 2-2	Mountfield, Ormondroyd	23,301
7		29	(a)	Tottenham H	L 1-2	Platt	34,939
8	Oct	6	(h)	Sunderland	W 3-0	Olney, Daley, Platt	26,017
9		20	(a)	Wimbledon	D 0-0		6,646
10		27	(h)	Leeds U	D 0-0		24,219
11	Nov	3	(a)	Chelsea	L 0-1		23,555
12		10	(h)	Nottingham F	D 1-1	Nielsen	25,797
13		17	(a)	Norwich C	L 0-2		17,243
14		24	(a)	Luton T	L 0-2		10,071
15	Dec	1	(h)	Sheffield U	W 2-1	Platt, Price	21,713
16		15	(a)	Southampton	D 1-1	Platt (pen)	16,604
17		23	(h)	Arsenal	D 0-0		22,687
18		26	(a)	Everton	L 0-1		27,804
19		29	(a)	Manchester U	D 1-1	Pallister (og)	47,485
20	Jan	1	(h)	Crystal Palace	W 2-0	Platt 2 (1 pen)	25,523
21		12	(h)	Liverpool	D 0-0		40,026
22		19	(a)	Coventry C	L 1-2	Platt	15,751
23	Feb	2	(h)	Derby Co	W 3-2	Cowans (pen), Cascarino, Yorke	21,852
24		23	(h)	Nottingham F	D 2-2	Cascarino, Mountfield	22,036
25	Mar	2	(a)	Sheffield U	L 1-2	Mountfield	22,074
26		9	(h)	Luton T	L 1-2	Cascarino	20,587
27		16	(h)	Tottenham H	W 3-2	Platt 3	32,638
28		23	(a)	Sunderland	W 3-1	Cascarino 2, Platt	21,099
29		30	(h)	Everton	D 2-2	Platt, Olney	27,660
30	Apr	3	(a)	Arsenal	L 0-5		41,868
31		6	(h)	Manchester U	D 1-1	Cascarino	33,307
32		10	(a)	QPR	L 1-2	Platt	11,539
33		13	(a)	Crystal Palace	D 0-0		18,331
34		20	(h)	Wimbledon	L 1-2	Olney	17,001
35		23	(h)	Manchester C	L 1-5	Platt (pen)	24,168
36	May	4	(a)	Leeds U	L 2-5	Nielsen, Mountfield	29,188
37		8	(h)	Norwich C	W 2-1	Bowen (og), Yorke	16,697
38		11	(h)	Chelsea	D 2-2	Cascarino, Platt (pen)	27,866

FINAL LEAGUE POSITION: 17th in Division One

Appearances

Sub. Appearances

Goals

Spink	Price	Gray	McGrath	Mountfield	Nielsen	Daley	Platt	Olney	Cowans	Cascarino	Gage	Gallacher	Yorke	Ormondroyd	Birch	Comyn	Blake	Butler	Callaghan	Penrice	
1	2	3	4	5	6	7	8	9	10	11											1
1	2	3	4	5	6	7	8		10	11	9										2
1	2	3	4	5*	6	7	8	12	10	11	9										3
1	2		4	5	6	7	8	9*	10	11		3	12								4
1	2	3	4	5	6	7	8		10	11	9										5
1	2	3	4	5	6	7	8	9*	10				12	11							6
1	2	3	4	5	6	7	8	9*	10				12	11							7
1	2	3	4	5	6	7	8	9†	10	14			12	11*							8
1	2	3		5	6	7	8		10	11			9*	12	4						9
1	2	3		5	6	7	8		10	11				9	4						10
1	2		4	5	6	7*	8		10	11		3	12	9							11
1	2	3	4	5	6	7	8	9	10	11											12
1	2	3	4	5	6	7	8	9	10	11											13
1	2	3	4	5†	6	7	8		10	11			14			12	9*				14
1	2	3	4		6	7	8	9*	10	12						11	5				15
1	2	3	4		6	7	8		10	11			14	9†		5*	12				16
1	2	3	4		6	7	8		10	11				9		5					17
1	2	3	4	5*	6	7	8		10	11			12	9							18
1	2	3	4	5	6	7*	8		10	11				9	12						19
	2	3	4	5	6		8		10	9			7	11				1			20
1	2		4		6		8		10	9	3			7		5			11		21
1	2	3	4		6		8		10	9	11†		14		12	7	5*				22
1	2	3	4	5	6	7			10	9	8		12					11*			23
1	2		4	5	6				10	9	3		7*			11	12	8			24
1	2	11	4	5	6		12		10	9	3		7				8*				25
1	2	3	4	5*	6†		8	12	10	9			14	7						11	26
1	2		4	5	6		8	12	10	9	3		7*							11	27
1	2		4	5	6		8		10	9	3					11			7		28
1	2		4	5	6*		8	12	10	9	3					11			7		29
1*	2		4	5			8		10	9	3					11	6	12	7		30
	2		4	5	6		8	7*	10	9	3			12		11		1			31
	2		4	5*	6		8	7	10	9	3					11		1		12	32
	2		4	5	6		8	7*	10	9	3					11		1		12	33
1	2			5	6	14	8	7	10	9	3					11†	4*			12	34
1	2		4		6	7	8	9	10	12	3					5*				11	35
1	2		4	5	6	7*	8		10	9	3			12						11	36
1	2		4	5	6		8		10	9	3			12				11*		7	37
1	2		4	5	6		8		10	9	3			11						7	38
34	38	22	35	32	37	22	35	13	38	33	20	2	8	13	6	9	6	4	2	9	
						1		5		3	1		10	5	2	2	1			3	
	1			4	2	2	19	3	1	9				2	1						

1991-92

								Attendance
1	Aug	17	(a)	Sheffield W	W	3-2	Staunton, Regis, Atkinson	36,749
2		21	(h)	Manchester U	L	0-1		39,995
3		24	(h)	Arsenal	W	3-1	Staunton (pen), Penrice, Daley	29,684
4		28	(a)	West Ham U	L	1-3	Daley	23,644
5		31	(a)	Southampton	D	1-1	Richardson	16,161
6	Sep	4	(h)	Crystal Palace	L	0-1		20,740
7		7	(h)	Tottenham H	D	0-0		33,096
8		14	(a)	Liverpool	D	1-1	Richardson	38,400
9		18	(a)	Chelsea	L	0-2		17,182
10		21	(h)	Nottingham F	W	3-1	Blake, Richardson, Yorke	28,506
11		28	(a)	Coventry C	L	0-1		17,851
12	Oct	5	(h)	Luton T	W	4-0	Richardson, Regis, Yorke, Mortimer	18,722
13		19	(a)	Everton	W	2-0	Regis, Daley	27,688
14		26	(h)	Wimbledon	W	2-1	Olney, Yorke	16,928
15	Nov	2	(a)	QPR	W	1-0	Yorke	10,642
16		16	(h)	Notts Co	W	1-0	Yorke	23,020
17		24	(h)	Leeds U	L	1-4	Yorke	23,713
18		30	(a)	Oldham A	L	2-3	Blake, Regis	15,370
19	Dec	7	(h)	Manchester C	W	3-1	Regis, Yorke, Daley	26,265
20		14	(a)	Sheffield U	L	0-2		18,401
21		26	(h)	West Ham U	W	3-1	Yorke, Daley, Richardson	31,959
22		28	(h)	Southampton	W	2-1	Regis, Yorke	23,094
23	Jan	1	(a)	Norwich C	L	1-2	Regis	15,318
24		11	(a)	Arsenal	D	0-0		31,413
25		18	(h)	Sheffield W	L	0-1		28,036
26		22	(a)	Manchester U	L	0-1		45,022
27	Feb	2	(h)	Everton	D	0-0		17,451
28		8	(a)	Wimbledon	L	0-2		5,534
29		22	(h)	Oldham A	W	1-0	Regis	20,509
30		29	(a)	Manchester C	L	0-2		28,268
31	Mar	3	(a)	Leeds U	D	0-0		28,896
32		10	(a)	Notts Co	D	0-0		8,389
33		14	(h)	QPR	L	0-1		19,630
34		21	(a)	Crystal Palace	D	0-0		15,368
35		28	(h)	Norwich C	W	1-0	Staunton	16,985
36		31	(h)	Sheffield U	D	1-1	Regis	15,745
37	Apr	4	(a)	Tottenham H	W	5-2	Richardson, Olney, Yorke, Daley, Regis	26,370
38		11	(h)	Liverpool	W	1-0	Daley	35,755
39		18	(a)	Nottingham F	L	0-2		22,800
40		20	(h)	Chelsea	W	3-1	Staunton, McGrath, Parker	19,269
41		25	(a)	Luton T	L	0-2		11,178
42	May	2	(h)	Coventry C	W	2-0	Regis, Yorke	31,984

FINAL LEAGUE POSITION: 7th in Division One

Appearances

Sub. Appearances

Goals

Spink	Mountfield	Staunton	Teale	McGrath	Richardson	Yorke	Regis	Atkinson	Cowans	Mortimer	Penrice	Olney	Ehiogu	Daley	Price	Kubicki	Ormondroyd	Nielsen	Blake	Sealey	Small	Parker	Froggatt	Breitkreutz	Carruthers	Barrett	Cox	Beinlich	Bosnich	
1	2	3	4	5	6	7	8	9*	10	11	12																			1
1	2	3	4	5	6	7	9		10	11*	8	12																		2
1		3*	4	5	6	14	9		10	11	8†		2	7	12															3
1			4	5	6	12	9		10	11	8		2	7	3*															4
1		3	4	5	6		8	9	10	11				7		2														5
1		3	4	5	6		9		10	11	8*			7		2		12												6
1		3	4	5	6		8	9	10	11				7		2														7
1		3	4	5	6	12	8	9†	10	11				7*		2		14												8
1		3	4	5	6	7	9*	10†	11	12	8					2		14												9
1		3	4	5	6	7	9†		14	12	8*					2		10	11											10
1		3	4	5	6	7	9	12		11*	10					2		8												11
1		3	4	5	6	7	8	9	10	12						2		11*												12
			4	5	6	11	8	9						7		2			10	1	3									13
		3	4	5	6	11	8	9						7		2			10	1										14
		3	4	5	6	11†	8	12				9*	14	7		2			10	1										15
		3	4	5	6	11*	8	12				9†	14	7		2			10	1										16
		3	4	5	6	11	8	9				12		7		2			10*	1										17
		3	4	5	6	11	9	10				12		7		2			7	1		8*								18
		3	4	5	6	11*	9					12		7		2			8	1		10								19
		3	4	5	6	11	9					12		7		2			8*	1		10								20
		3	4	5	6	11*	9							7		2			8	1		10	12							21
		3*	4	5	6	11	9							7		2	12		8	1		10								22
			4	5	6	11	9					12		7	3	2			8*	1		10								23
			4	5	6	11	9							7		2				1	3	10	8							24
		3	4	5	6	11	9							7		2				1	8*	10		12						25
		3*	4	5	6	11	9							7		2				1	8	10	12							26
		3	4	5	6	11	9*					12		7		2				1		10	8							27
		11	4	5	6		9							7				2		1	3*	10		12		8				28
		3	4	5	6		9											2		1		10	11	8	7					29
		3	4	5	6	8*	9							7				2		1		10	11	12		2				30
1		3	4	5	6		9	10						7					11			8				2				31
1		3	4	5	6	10*	9					12										8	11			2	7			32
1		3	4	5	6	14	10					12		9†								8		11*		2	7			33
1		3	4	5	6	11*	10					12		9								8			7	2				34
1		3	4	5	6	11*	9	10				14		12								8		7†		2				35
1		3	4	5	6	12	9	10						7								8*		11		2				36
1		3	4	5	6	11†	9	10				12										8		7*		2	14			37
1			4		6		9	10					5	7							3	8		11*		2	12			38
1		3	4	5	6	9†		10						7								8		11*		2	12	14		39
1		3	4	5	6		9							7					11*			8				2	10	12		40
		3	4	5	6	10*	9	12						7								8	11			2			1	41
1		3	4	5	6	10*	9					12		7					11			8				2				42
23	2	37	42	41	42	27	39	11	10	10	5	14	4	29	2	23		3	14	18	8	25	6	7	2	13	4		1	
							5		3	2	2	3	6	4	5	1		1	3			3	1	1		3	2			
		4		1	6	11	11	1		1	1	2		7				2			1									

65

1992-93

#	Month	Date		Opponent	Result	Score	Scorers	Attendance
1	Aug	15	(a)	Ipswich T	D	1-1	Atkinson	16,818
2		19	(h)	Leeds U	D	1-1	Atkinson	29,151
3		22	(h)	Southampton	D	1-1	Atkinson	17,894
4		25	(a)	Everton	L	0-1		22,372
5		29	(a)	Sheffield U	W	2-0	Parker 2	18,773
6	Sep	2	(h)	Chelsea	L	1-3	Richardson	19,125
7		5	(h)	Crystal Palace	W	3-0	Yorke, Staunton, Froggatt	17,120
8		13	(a)	Leeds U	D	1-1	Parker	27,817
9		19	(h)	Liverpool	W	4-2	Saunders 2, Atkinson, Parker	37,863
10		26	(a)	Middlesbrough	W	3-2	Saunders 2, Atkinson	20,905
11	Oct	3	(a)	Wimbledon	W	3-2	Saunders 2, Atkinson	6,849
12		19	(h)	Blackburn R	D	0-0		30,398
13		24	(a)	Oldham Ath	D	1-1	Atkinson	13,457
14	Nov	1	(h)	QPR	W	2-0	Saunders, Atkinson	20,140
15		7	(h)	Manchester U	W	1-0	Atkinson	39,063
16		21	(a)	Tottenham H	D	0-0		32,852
17		28	(h)	Norwich C	L	2-3	Houghton, Parker	28,837
18	Dec	5	(a)	Sheffield W	W	2-1	Atkinson 2	29,964
19		12	(h)	Nottingham F	W	2-1	Regis, McGrath	29,015
20		19	(a)	Manchester C	D	1-1	Parker	23,525
21		26	(a)	Coventry C	L	0-3		24,245
22		28	(h)	Arsenal	W	1-0	Saunders (pen)	35,170
23	Jan	9	(a)	Liverpool	W	2-1	Parker, Saunders	40,826
24		17	(h)	Middlesbrough	W	5-1	Parker, McGrath, Yorke, Saunders, Teale	19,977
25		27	(h)	Sheffield U	W	3-1	McGrath, Saunders, Richardson	20,266
26		30	(a)	Southampton	L	0-2		19,087
27	Feb	6	(h)	Ipswich T	W	2-0	Yorke, Saunders	25,395
28		10	(a)	Crystal Palace	L	0-1		12,270
29		13	(a)	Chelsea	W	1-0	Houghton	20,081
30		20	(h)	Everton	W	2-1	Cox, Barrett	32,913
31		27	(h)	Wimbledon	W	1-0	Yorke	34,496
32	Mar	10	(h)	Tottenham H	D	0-0		37,727
33		14	(a)	Manchester U	D	1-1	Staunton	36,163
34		20	(h)	Sheffield W	W	2-0	Yorke 2	38,024
35		24	(a)	Norwich C	L	0-1		19,528
36	Apr	4	(a)	Nottingham F	W	1-0	McGrath	26,742
37		10	(h)	Coventry C	D	0-0		38,543
38		12	(a)	Arsenal	W	1-0	Daley	27,123
39		18	(h)	Manchester C	W	3-1	Saunders, Parker (pen), Houghton	33,108
40		21	(a)	Blackburn R	L	0-3		15,127
41	May	2	(h)	Oldham Ath	L	0-1		37,247
42		9	(a)	QPR	L	1-2	Daley	18,904

FINAL LEAGUE POSITION: 2nd in Premier Division

Appearances

Sub. Appearances

Goals

Spink	Barrett	Staunton	Teale	McGrath	Richardson	Daley	Parker	Houghton	Atkinson	Froggatt	Regis	Yorke	Ehiogu	McAvennie	Saunders	Blake	Small	Farrell	Bosnich	Cox	Breitkreutz	Beinlich	Carruthers	
1	2	3	4	5	6*	7	8	9	10	11	12													1
1	2	3	4	5	6	7	8	9	10		12	11*												2
1	2	3	4	5	6		8	7	10	11*		9†	12	14										3
1	2	3	4	5	6	7	8*	9	10	11	12													4
1	2	3	4	5	6		8	7	10	11	9*		12											5
1	2	3	4	5	6		8	7	10	11	9*			12										6
1	2	3	4	5	6		8	7	10	11		9*		12										7
1	2	3	4	5	6		8	7	10	11					9									8
1	2	3	4	5	6		8	7	10	11					9									9
1	2	3	4	5	6		8†	7	10	11*		12		14	9									10
1	2	3	4	5	6		8	7	10	11*		12			9									11
1	2	3	4	5	6		8	7	10	11*					9		12							12
1	2	3	4	5	6			7	10			8*			9		11	12						13
1	2	3	4	5	6		8	7	10†			14			9		12	11*						14
1	2	3	4	5	6		8	7	10						9		11							15
1	2	3	4†	5	6		8*	7	10				12	14	9		11							16
1	2	3		5	6		8	7	10			12	4*		9		11							17
	2	3		5	6		8		10			7			9		11		1	4				18
1	2	3	4	5	6		8	7	10						9					11				19
1	2	3	4	5	6		8	7	10*			11			9					12				20
1	2	3	4	5	6		8*	7	10†						9		11			12		14		21
1	2	3	4	5	6		8	7		11*		10			9					12				22
1	2	3	4	5	6		8	7	10†	14*		11			9					12				23
1	2	3	4	5*	6		8	7		11†		10			9					12		14		24
1	2	3	4	5	6		8					10†			9		11			12	7*	14		25
1	2	3	4	5	6		8					10			9		11†			12	7*	14		26
	2	3	4	5	6		8	7		11*		10†			9				1	12		14		27
	2	3	4	5	6		8*	7		11		10			9				1	12				28
	2	3	4	5	6		8*	7	10†	11		14			9				1	12				29
	2	3	4	5	6			7				10			9				1	8		11		30
	2	3	4	5	6			7		11		10			9				1	8				31
	2	3	4	5	6	11*	8	7			12	10			9				1					32
	2	3	4	5	6	12	8*	7				10			9		11		1					33
	2	3	4	5	6		8	7		11		10			9				1					34
	2	3	4	5	6	12	8*	7		11		10			9				1					35
	2	3	4	5	6	12	8	7	10			11*			9				1					36
	2	3	4	5	6	12	8	7	10			11*			9				1					37
	2	3	4	5	6	11*		7	10						9		12		1	8				38
	2	3		5	6	11	8*	7	10						9		12		1	4				39
	2	3	4	5	6	11		7	10			12			9		8*		1					40
	2	3	4	5	6	12	8*	7	10			11			9				1					41
	2	3	4	5	6	11	8	7†	10						9*				1	12		14		42
25	42	42	39	42	42	8	37	39	28	16	7	22	1		35		10	1	17	6	2	1		
					5					1	6	5	3	3		1	4	1		9	1	6	1	
	1	2	1	4	2	2	9	3	11	1	1	6			13					1				

1993-94

#	Month	Date		Opponent	Res	Score	Scorers	Att
1	Aug	14	(h)	QPR	W	4-1	Atkinson 2, Saunders, Staunton	32,944
2		18	(a)	Sheffield W	D	0-0		28,450
3		21	(a)	Wimbledon	D	2-2	Richardson, McGrath	7,564
4		23	(h)	Manchester U	L	1-2	Atkinson	39,624
5		28	(h)	Tottenham H	W	1-0	Staunton (pen)	32,498
6		31	(a)	Everton	W	1-0	Whittingham	24,067
7	Sep	11	(h)	Coventry C	D	0-0		31,181
8		18	(a)	Ipswich T	W	2-1	Saunders, Townsend	16,858
9		25	(a)	Oldham Ath	D	1-1	Saunders	12,836
10	Oct	2	(h)	Newcastle U	L	0-2		37,336
11		16	(a)	West Ham U	D	0-0		20,416
12		23	(h)	Chelsea	W	1-0	Atkinson	29,706
13		30	(a)	Swindon T	W	2-1	Teale, Atkinson	16,332
14	Nov	6	(a)	Arsenal	W	2-1	Whittingham, Townsend	31,773
15		20	(h)	Sheffield U	W	1-0	Whittingham	24,686
16		24	(h)	Southampton	L	0-2		16,180
17		28	(a)	Liverpool	L	1-2	Atkinson	38,484
18	Dec	4	(a)	QPR	D	2-2	Richardson, Parker	14,915
19		8	(h)	Sheffield W	D	2-2	Cox, Saunders (pen)	20,304
20		11	(h)	Wimbledon	L	0-1		17,940
21		19	(a)	Manchester U	L	1-3	Cox	44,499
22		29	(a)	Norwich C	W	2-1	Houghton, Saunders	20,650
23	Jan	1	(h)	Blackburn R	L	0-1		40,903
24		15	(h)	West Ham U	W	3-1	Richardson, Atkinson 2	28,869
25		22	(a)	Chelsea	D	1-1	Saunders	18,348
26	Feb	6	(h)	Leeds U	W	1-0	Townsend	26,919
27		12	(h)	Swindon T	W	5-0	Saunders 3 (2 pens), Froggatt, Richardson	27,637
28		22	(h)	Manchester C	D	0-0		19,254
29	Mar	2	(a)	Tottenham H	D	1-1	Parker	17,452
30		6	(a)	Coventry C	W	1-0	Daley	14,323
31		12	(h)	Ipswich T	L	0-1		23,732
32		16	(a)	Leeds U	L	0-2		33,126
33		19	(h)	Oldham Ath	L	1-2	Redmond (og)	21,214
34		30	(h)	Everton	D	0-0		36,044
35	Apr	2	(a)	Manchester C	L	0-3		26,075
36		4	(h)	Norwich C	D	0-0		25,416
37		11	(a)	Blackburn R	L	0-1		19,287
38		16	(a)	Sheffield U	W	2-1	Richardson, Fenton	18,402
39		23	(h)	Arsenal	L	1-2	Houghton	31,580
40		27	(a)	Newcastle U	L	1-5	Beinlich	32,217
41		30	(a)	Southampton	L	1-4	Saunders	18,803
42	May	7	(h)	Liverpool	W	2-1	Yorke 2	45,347

FINAL LEAGUE POSITION: 10th in Premiership

Appearances

Sub. Appearances

Goals

Spink	Barrett	Staunton	Teale	McGrath	Richardson	Houghton	Townsend	Saunders	Atkinson	Daley	Cowans	Froggatt	Small	Parker	Whittingham	Cox	Bosnich	Ehiogu	Kubicki	Beinlich	Yorke	Farrell	Fenton	Breitkreuz	
1	2	3	4	5	6	7*	8	9	10	11	12														1
1	2	3	4	5	6		8*	9	10	7	12	11													2
1	2	3	4	5	6	7		9	10		8	11													3
1	2	3†	4	5	6	7*		9	10			14	11	8	12										4
1	2	3	4	5	6	7		9	10	11*				8	12										5
1	2	3	4	5	6		8	9*	10		7				11	12									6
1	2	3	4	5	6	12	8	9	10		7				11*										7
1	2	3	4	5	6	12	8	9	10*	14	7				11†										8
		3	4	5	6	7	8	9			10				11	2	1								9
1		3	4	5	6	12	8	9	10	14	7*				11†	2									10
			4	5	6	7	8	9	10	11		3				2	1								11
	2		4		6		8	9	5	11	7		12	10*		1	3								12
1	2		4		6	9	8†		5	12			11	10	7*	3		14							13
14	2		4	5	6	7*	8	9	10	11		3		12			1†								14
	2		4	5	6†		8	9	10	11		3*	12	7			1	14							15
	2		4	5	6	12	8	9		11			10	7			1		3*						16
	2			5	6	7	8	9	10			3*	11	12		4	1								17
	2		4	5	6	7	8*	9	10	12				11		3	1								18
	3		4	5		7		9	10		6			8		2	1				11				19
	3		4	5		7†		9	10*		6			8	12	2	1	14			11				20
	2		4	5	6		9*	10	12			7		8	11	3	1								21
	2	3	4	5	6	7	8	9						10*	11		1				12				22
	2	3*	12	5	6	7	8	9						10		4	1				14	11†			23
	2	3*	4	5	6	7	8	9	10	11					12		1								24
	2	3	4	5	6	7	8	9	10	11							1								25
	2	3*	4	5	6	7†	8	9	10	11					12		1				14				26
	2		5*	6	4	8†	9	10	11	7						3	1	12			14				27
	2		4		6		8	12				3	10	11*			1	5			7		9		28
	2		4	5	6			9	10	7				8	11	3*	1				12				29
	3		4		6		8	9		7					11	2	1	5			10				30
	3		4		6	8†	9	10	7						11*	2	1	5			12	14			31
	3		4	5	6			9	10†	11	7*		8			2	1				12	14			32
	2	3	4	5	6	7	9*			11			8				1				12	10			33
	2	3	4		6	7	9			11			8				1	5			10*	12			34
	2	3	4		6		8	9	10	7				11*			1	5			12	10			35
	2	3	4		6		8	9	10	7							1	5			12	11*			36
	2	3	4		6	12	8	9*	10	11							1	5				7			37
1	2	3	4		6	7	8			12								5		10	11*	9			38
1	3		4		6	7	8			10						2		5				11	9		39
1	2	3	4*		6	7	8			12								5		10		11	9†	14	40
1	2	3	5†	6*	7	8	9			12			14			4				10			11		41
	2	3		5	6	7	8	9	11*			14				4	1			10†	12				42
14	39	24	37	30	40	25	32	37	29	19	9	8	8	17	13	16	28	14	1	6	2	4	9	1	
1			1			5		1		8	2	1	1	2	5	4		3	1	1	10		3	1	
		2	1	1	5	2	3	10	8	1		1		2	3	2				1	2		1		

69

1994-95

1	Aug	20	(a)	Everton	D	2-2	Fashanu, Saunders	35,552
2		24	(h)	Southampton	D	1-1	Saunders	24,179
3		27	(h)	Crystal Palace	D	1-1	Staunton	23,305
4		29	(a)	Coventry C	W	1-0	Yorke	12,218
5	Sep	10	(h)	Ipswich T	W	2-0	Staunton, Saunders	22,241
6		17	(a)	West Ham U	L	0-1		18,326
7		24	(a)	Blackburn R	L	1-3	Ehiogu	22,694
8	Oct	1	(h)	Newcastle U	L	0-2		29,960
9		8	(a)	Liverpool	L	2-3	Whittingham, Staunton	32,158
10		15	(h)	Norwich C	D	1-1	Saunders	22,468
11		22	(h)	Nottingham F	L	0-2		29,217
12		29	(a)	QPR	L	0-2		16,073
13	Nov	6	(h)	Manchester U	L	1-2	Atkinson	32,136
14		9	(a)	Wimbledon	L	3-4	Parker, Saunders 2	6,221
15		19	(a)	Tottenham H	W	4-3	Atkinson, Fenton 2, Saunders	26,899
16		27	(h)	Sheffield W	D	1-1	Atkinson	25,082
17	Dec	3	(a)	Leicester C	D	1-1	Whittingham	20,896
18		10	(h)	Everton	D	0-0		29,678
19		19	(a)	Southampton	L	1-2	Houghton	13,874
20		26	(a)	Arsenal	D	0-0		34,452
21		28	(h)	Chelsea	W	3-0	Sinclair (og), Yorke, Taylor	32,901
22		31	(a)	Manchester C	D	2-2	Brightwell I (og), Saunders	22,513
23	Jan	2	(h)	Leeds U	D	0-0		35,038
24		14	(h)	QPR	W	2-1	Fashanu, Ehiogu	26,578
25		21	(a)	Nottingham F	W	2-1	Fashanu, Saunders	24,598
26		25	(h)	Tottenham H	W	1-0	Saunders	40,017
27	Feb	4	(a)	Manchester U	L	0-1		43,795
28		11	(h)	Wimbledon	W	7-1	Reeves (og), Johnson 3, Saunders 2 (1 pen), Yorke	23,982
29		18	(a)	Sheffield W	W	2-1	Saunders 2	24,063
30		22	(h)	Leicester C	D	4-4	Saunders, Staunton, Yorke, Johnson	30,825
31		25	(a)	Newcastle U	L	1-3	Townsend	34,637
32	Mar	4	(h)	Blackburn R	L	0-1		40,114
33		6	(h)	Coventry C	D	0-0		26,186
34		18	(h)	West Ham U	L	0-2		28,682
35	Apr	1	(a)	Ipswich T	W	1-0	Swailes (og)	15,895
36		4	(a)	Crystal Palace	D	0-0		12,949
37		15	(a)	Chelsea	L	0-1		17,015
38		17	(h)	Arsenal	L	0-4		32,005
39		29	(a)	Leeds U	L	0-1		32,973
40	May	3	(h)	Manchester C	D	1-1	Ehiogu	30,133
41		6	(h)	Liverpool	W	2-0	Yorke 2	40,154
42		14	(a)	Norwich C	D	1-1	Staunton	19,374

FINAL LEAGUE POSITION: 18th in F.A. Carling Premiership

Appearances

Sub. Appearances

Goals

Bosnich	Richardson	Staunton	Townsend	McGrath	Ehiogu	Houghton	Fashanu	Saunders	Parker	Yorke	King	Atkinson	Barrett	Spink	Teale	Lamptey	Fenton	Whittingham	Small	Boden	Taylor	Johnson	Charles	Carr	Wright	No.
1	2	3*	4	5	6	7	8	9	10	11	12															1
1	2		4	5	6	7	8*	9	10†	11	3	12	14													2
1	6	3	11	5	4	7*	8	9		12		10	2													3
1	6	11	10	5	4		8	9		7	3		2													4
	6	11	10	5	4		8*	9		7	3	12	2	1												5
1	6	3	10		5	7	8	9		11*		12	2		4											6
1	6	3	8	5	7			9		11		10	2		4*	12†	14									7
		12	8	5	4	7*			6	11	3		2	1			14	9†	10							8
1		3	8*	5	4	7†		9	6	11	12		2				14		10							9
1	6	11*		5	4	12		9	8	7	3	10†	2					14								10
	6	8		5	4	7		9	12	11	3†		2	1			10*	14								11
1	6*	3	8	5	4			9		11	7		2			10	12									12
	6	11*	8	5	4	7†		9	14	12	3	10	2	1												13
1	12	8		5	4	7*		9†	6	11	3	10	2				14									14
1	6			5	4	7		9	8		3	10*	2			12	11									15
1	6			5	4	7		9	8		3	10*	2				11	12								16
		12		5		7		9	6	11†			2	1	4		8*	10	3	14						17
	6			5		7		8		11*			2	1	4	12	9	10	3							18
	6			5		7	8	9	10	12	11*		2	1	4			3								19
	6	3	10	12	5	7	8	9*					2	1	4						11					20
	6	3*	8	12	5	7				11			2	1	4						10					21
	6	3†	8*	12	5	7	14	9		11			2	1	4						10					22
	6	3		5	8	7*	12	9		11			2	1	4						10					23
1		3		5	6	12	8*	9		7			2		4						10	11				24
1		3		5	6	12	8	9		7*			2		4						10	11†	14			25
1		3	8	5	6	12		9		7†			2		4						10	11*	14			26
1	6	11		5		12	8†	9		7*					4			3			10	14	2			27
1	6	11		5				9		7					4			3			10	8	2			28
1	6	11		5	4			9		7					3						10	8	2			29
1	6	11		5	4			9		7†		12			3						10	8*	2	14		30
1	6	11		5	4			9		7		12			3*						10	8	2			31
1	6	11*		5	4	12		9		7					3		14				10	8†	2			32
1	6			5	4	7†		9		11					3		12				10	8*	2	14		33
1	6	11		5	14	12		9		7†					4						10	8*	2		3	34
1	11	7		5	6			9*		12	8†				4		14				10		2		3	35
1	11*	8		5	6					7	9				4		12				10		2		3	36
1	6	11		5	2			9		7	8†				4		12				10	14			3*	37
1	3	11		5	2			9		7	10				4						6	8				38
1†	11	8*		5	6			9		7			15		4		12				10		2		3	39
1	11	8		5	6			9		7					4						10		2		3	40
1	11*	8		5	6			9		7					4		12				10		2		3	41
	11	8		5	6			9*		7	12			1	4		10*					14	2		3	42
30	18	34	32	36	38	19	11	39	12	33	13	11	24	12	28	1	7	4	5		22	11	14		8	
	1	1		4	1	7	2		2	4	3	5	1	1		5	10	3		1		3	2	2		
		5	1		3	1	3	15	1	6		3					2	2			1	4				

71

1995-96

1	Aug	19	(h)	Manchester U	W	3-1	Taylor, Draper, Yorke (pen)		34,655
2		23	(a)	Tottenham H	W	1-0	Ehiogu		26,598
3		26	(a)	Leeds U	L	0-2			35,086
4		30	(h)	Bolton W	W	1-0	Yorke		31,770
5	Sep	9	(a)	Blackburn R	D	1-1	Milosevic		27,084
6		16	(h)	Wimbledon	W	2-0	Draper, Taylor		26,928
7		23	(h)	Nottingham F	D	1-1	Townsend		33,972
8		30	(a)	Coventry C	W	3-0	Yorke, Milosevic 2		21,004
9	Oct	14	(h)	Chelsea	L	0-1			34,922
10		21	(a)	Arsenal	L	0-2			38,271
11		28	(h)	Everton	W	1-0	Yorke		32,792
12	Nov	4	(a)	West Ham U	W	4-1	Milosevic 2, Johnson, Yorke		23,637
13		18	(h)	Newcastle U	D	1-1	Johnson		39,167
14		20	(a)	Southampton	W	1-0	Johnson		13,582
15		25	(a)	Manchester C	L	0-1			28,027
16	Dec	2	(h)	Arsenal	S	1-1	Yorke		37,770
17		10	(a)	Nottingham F	S	1-1	Yorke		25,790
18		16	(h)	Coventry C	W	4-1	Johnson, Milosevic 3		28,486
19		23	(a)	QPR	L	0-1			14,778
20	Jan	1	(a)	Middlesbrough	W	2-0	Wright, Johnson		28,523
21		13	(a)	Manchester U	D	0-0			42,667
22		21	(h)	Tottenham H	W	2-1	McGrath, Yorke		35,666
23		31	(h)	Liverpool	L	0-2			39,332
24	Feb	3	(h)	Leeds U	W	3-0	Yorke 2, Wright		35,982
25		10	(a)	Bolton W	W	2-0	Yorke 2		18,099
26		24	(a)	Wimbledon	D	3-3	Reeves (og), Yorke (pen), Cunningham (og)		12,193
27		28	(h)	Blackburn R	W	2-0	Joachim, Southgate		28,008
28	Mar	3	(a)	Liverpool	L	0-3			39,508
29		6	(h)	Sheffield W	W	3-2	Milosevic 2, Townsend		27,893
30		9	(h)	QPR	W	4-2	Milosevic, Yorke 2, Yates (og)		28,221
31		16	(a)	Sheffield W	L	0-2			22,964
32		19	(h)	Middlesbrough	D	0-0			23,933
33	Apr	6	(a)	Chelsea	W	2-1	Milosevic, Yorke		23,530
34		8	(h)	Southampton	W	3-0	Taylor, Charles, Yorke		34,059
35		14	(a)	Newcastle U	L	0-1			36,546
36		17	(h)	West Ham U	D	1-1	McGrath		26,768
37		27	(h)	Manchester C	L	0-1			39,336
38	May	5	(a)	Everton	L	0-1			40,127

FINAL LEAGUE POSITION: 4th in the F.A. Premiership

Appearances

Sub. Appearances

Goals

Bosnich M	Charles G	Wright A	Southgate G	McGrath P	Ehiogu U	Taylor I	Draper M	Milosevic S	Townsend A	Yorke D	Johnson T	Scimeca R	Fenton G	Staunton S	Tiler C	Spink N	Hendrie L	Farrelly G	Joachim J	Carr F	Davis N	Murray S	Browne P	No.
1	2	3	4	5	6	7	8	9*	10	11†	12	13												1
1	2	3	4	5	6	7	8	9	10	11														2
1		3	4	5	6	2	8	9	7	11	10*		12											3
1	2	3	4	5	6	7	8	9	10	11														4
1	2	3	4	5	6	7	8	9	10	11														5
1	2	3	4	5	6	7	8	9	10	11														6
1	2	3	4	5	6	7	8	9*	10	11	12													7
1	2	3	4		5	7	8	9	10	11				6										8
1	2	3	4	5	6	7	8	9*		10	12		13	11†										9
1	2	3	4	5†	6	7	8°	14	10	9	12		13	11*										10
1	2	3	4		5	7	8	9	10	11	12			6*										11
1	2	3	4	5	6	7	8	9	10*	11	12													12
1	2	3	4	5	6	7	8	9		11	10													13
1	2	3	4	5	6	7	8	9		11	10													14
1	2	3	4	5	6	7*	8	9†		11	10	13		12										15
1	2	3	4	5	6		8	9	11	7	10													16
1	2	3	4		6	7	8	9		11	10			5										17
1*	2	3	4	5†	6	7	8	9	12	11*	10	13			15									18
1	2	3	4	5*	6	7†	8°	9	11		10	12			13	14								19
1	2	3	4		6		8	9	7	11	10			5										20
1	2	3	4	5	6	7	8	9	11		10*	12												21
1	2	3	4	5	6	12	8	9	11	7	10*													22
1	2	3	4	5*	6		8	9	11	7	10			12										23
1	2	3	4	5		7	8	9	10*	11				6				12						24
1	2	3	4		5		8	9	11	7	10			6										25
1	2	3	4	12	5		8	9†	11	7		10*		6					13					26
1	2	3	4		5		8*	9	10	11		12		6				13	7†					27
1	2	3	4		5			9	10	11		7		6*				8	12					28
1	2	3	4	5	6			9	10	11		7							8					29
1	2	3	4†	5	6		8	9	10*	11		7						12	13					30
1	2	3		5	6		8	9	10	11		4*							12	7				31
1		3		5			8		10	11				6			7	12	9†		13	2*	4	32
1	2	3		5	4	7	8	9	10	11	12			6*										33
1	2	3		5*	6	7	8	9	4	11	10	12												34
1	2	3		5	6	7	8	9	4	11†	10*	12	13											35
1	2*	3		5	6	7	8	9	4	11†	10	12	13											36
1		3		5	4		8	9	11		10			6					7*		12	2		37
1		3	4		5		8	9	10	7*			11	12								2	6	38
38	34	38	31	29	36	24	36	36	32	35	17	7		11	1		2	1	4	1		3	2	
				1		1		1	1		6	10	3	2		2	1	4	7		2			
	1	2	1	2	1	3	2	12	2	17	5								1					

1996-97

1	Aug	17	(a)	Sheffield W	L	1-2	Johnson	26,861
2		21	(h)	Blackburn R	W	1-0	Southgate	32,457
3		24	(h)	Derby Co	W	2-0	Joachim, Johnson (pen)	34,646
4	Sep	4	(a)	Everton	W	1-0	Ehiogu	39,115
5		7	(h)	Arsenal	D	2-2	Milosevic 2	37,944
6		15	(a)	Chelsea	D	1-1	Townsend	27,729
7		21	(h)	Manchester U	D	0-0		39,339
8		30	(a)	Newcastle U	L	3-4	Yorke 3	36,400
9	Oct	12	(a)	Tottenham H	L	0-1		32,840
10		19	(h)	Leeds U	W	2-0	Yorke, Johnson	39,051
11		26	(a)	Sunderland	L	0-1		21,032
12	Nov	2	(h)	Nottingham F	W	2-0	Tiler, Yorke	35,310
13		16	(h)	Leicester C	L	1-3	Yorke	36,193
14		23	(a)	Coventry C	W	2-1	Joachim, Staunton	21,335
15		30	(h)	Middlesbrough	W	1-0	Yorke (pen)	39,053
16	Dec	4	(a)	West Ham U	W	2-0	Ehiogu, Yorke	19,105
17		7	(a)	Southampton	W	1-0	Townsend	15,232
18		22	(h)	Wimbledon	W	5-0	Yorke 2, Milosevic, Taylor, Blackwell (og)	28,875
19		26	(h)	Chelsea	L	0-2		39,339
20		28	(a)	Arsenal	D	2-2	Milosevic, Yorke	38,130
21	Jan	1	(a)	Manchester U	D	0-0		55,133
22		11	(h)	Newcastle U	D	2-2	Yorke, Milosevic	39,339
23		18	(a)	Liverpool	L	0-3		40,489
24		29	(h)	Sheffield W	L	0-1		26,726
25	Feb	1	(h)	Sunderland	W	1-0	Milosevic	32,491
26		19	(h)	Coventry C	W	2-1	Yorke 2	30,409
27		22	(a)	Nottingham F	D	0-0		25,239
28	Mar	2	(h)	Liverpool	W	1-0	Taylor	39,339
29		5	(a)	Leicester C	L	0-1		20,626
30		15	(h)	West Ham U	D	0-0		35,992
31		22	(a)	Blackburn R	W	2-0	Johnson, Yorke	24,274
32	Apr	5	(h)	Everton	W	3-1	Milosevic, Staunton, Yorke	39,339
33		9	(a)	Wimbledon	W	2-0	Milosevic, Wright	9,015
34		12	(a)	Derby Co	L	1-2	Joachim	18,071
35		19	(h)	Tottenham H	D	1-1	Yorke	39,339
36		22	(a)	Leeds U	D	0-0		26,884
37	May	3	(a)	Middlesbrough	L	2-3	Ehiogu, Milosevic	30,012
38		11	(h)	Southampton	W	1-0	Dryden (og)	39,339

FINAL LEAGUE POSITION: 5th in the F.A. Premiership

Appearances

Sub. Appearances

Goals

74

Oakes M	Murray S	Staunton S	Southgate G	Ehiogu U	Townsend A	Taylor I	Draper M	Yorke D	Johnson T	Wright A	Joachim J	Scimeca R	Curcic S	Nelson F	Milosevic S	Bosnich M	Tiler C	Hendrie L	Hughes D	Farrelly G	
1	2*	3	4	5	6	7	8	9	10	11	12										1
1		3	4	5	6	2	8	9	10*	11	7	12									2
1		3	4	5	6	2	8	9*	10	11	12		7†	13							3
1		6	4	5	7	12	8	11	13	3		14	10*	2°	9†						4
1		6	4	5	7	13	8	11	12	3			10	2†	9*						5
1		6	4	5	7	12	8	11	13	3			10*	2	9†						6
1		6	4	5	7	12	8	11		3			10*	2	9						7
1		6	4	5		7	8	11		3			10	2	9						8
		6		5	10°	7	8*	11	13	3	12		4	2	9†	1	14				9
		6†		5	11	7		9	10*	3	12	13	8	2		1	4				10
15			4	5	11	2	8†	9	10	3	12		7*			1°	6	13			11
1			4	5	11	7		9	10	3			8	2			6				12
1			4	5	11	7	12	9	10	3		13	8†	2*			6				13
1		6	4	5	11	12	8°	10		3	9†	13	7*	2	14						14
1		6		5	10	7	8	11		3			4	2	9						15
1		6		5	10	7	8	11		3			4	2	9						16
1		6		5	10	7	8	11*		3	12		4	2	9						17
		6†		5	10	7	8*	11		3		12	4	2	9	1		13			18
		6		5	10	7	8†	11	12	3		13	4	2	9*	1					19
		6		5	10	7	8*	11	12	3			4	2	9	1					20
		6		5	10	7*	8	11	12	3				2	9	1	4				21
		6	8	5		7		11*	10	3	12	13	2†		9	1	4				22
			4	5		7		11	10	3			2	8	9	1	6				23
		11	4	5		7				3	12	10	8†	2	9	1	6*	13			24
		11	10	5		7				3		4	8*	2	9	1	6	12			25
		6	4	5	10	7	8	11		3				2	9	1					26
		6*	4	5	10	7	8	11		3			12	2	9	1					27
		6*	4	5	10	7	8	11		3				2	9	1		12			28
			4	5	10	7	8†	11	12	3		13		2	9*	1		6			29
			4	5	10	7	8†	11	12	3		9*		2		1		13	6		30
		6		5	10	7	8	11	12	3			4	2	9*	1					31
1		6†	4	5		7*	8	11		3			12	2	9			13	10		32
1			4	5	10	7	8	11		3				2	9			6			33
1			4	5	10	7	8*	11		3		13	12	2	9			6†			34
1		6	4†	5	10	7	8*	11		3			12	2	9			13			35
		6	4	5	10*	7		11		3			8	2	9	1			12		36
15		6	4	5	10	7		11		3	12		8*	2	9†	1°			13		37
		11	4	5	10	7		8		3			6		9						38
18	1	30	28	38	34	29	28	37	10	38	3	11	17	33	29	20	9		4	1	
2						5	1		10		12	6	5	1	1		2	4	3	2	
		2	1	3	2	2		17	4	1	3				9		1				

1997-98

1	Aug	9	(a)	Leicester C	L	0-1		20,304
2		13	(h)	Blackburn R	L	0-4		37,122
3		23	(a)	Newcastle U	L	0-1		36,783
4		27	(a)	Tottenham H	L	2-3	Yorke, Collymore	26,316
5		30	(h)	Leeds U	W	1-0	Yorke	39,027
6	Sep	13	(a)	Barnsley	W	3-0	Ehiogu, Draper, Taylor	18,649
7		20	(h)	Derby Co	W	2-1	Yorke, Joachim	35,444
8		22	(a)	Liverpool	L	0-3		34,843
9		27	(h)	Sheffield W	D	2-2	Staunton, Taylor	32,044
10	Oct	4	(a)	Bolton W	W	1-0	Milosevic	24,196
11		18	(h)	Wimbledon	L	1-2	Taylor	32,087
12		26	(a)	Arsenal	D	0-0		38,061
13	Nov	1	(h)	Chelsea	L	0-2		39,372
14		8	(a)	Crystal Palace	D	1-1	Joachim	21,097
15		22	(h)	Everton	W	2-1	Milosevic, Ehiogu	36,389
16		29	(a)	West Ham U	L	1-2	Yorke	24,976
17	Dec	6	(h)	Coventry C	W	3-0	Collymore, Hendrie, Joachim	33,250
18		15	(a)	Manchester U	L	0-1		55,175
19		20	(h)	Southampton	D	1-1	Taylor	29,343
20		26	(h)	Tottenham H	W	4-1	Draper 2, Collymore 2	38,644
21		28	(a)	Leeds U	W	1-1	Milosevic	36,909
22	Jan	10	(h)	Leicester C	D	1-1	Joachim	36,429
23		17	(a)	Blackburn R	L	0-5		24,834
24	Feb	1	(h)	Newcastle U	L	0-1		38,266
25		7	(a)	Derby Co	W	1-0	Yorke	30,251
26		18	(h)	Manchester U	L	0-2		39,372
27		21	(a)	Wimbledon	L	1-2	Milosevic	13,131
28		28	(h)	Liverpool	W	2-1	Collymore 2	39,372
29	Mar	8	(a)	Chelsea	W	1-0	Joachim	33,018
30		11	(h)	Barnsley	L	0-1		29,519
31		14	(h)	Crystal Palace	W	3-1	Taylor, Milosevic 2 (1 pen)	33,781
32		28	(a)	Everton	W	4-1	Joachim, Charles, Yorke 2 (1 pen)	36,471
33	Apr	4	(h)	West Ham U	W	2-0	Joachim, Milosevic	39,372
34		11	(a)	Coventry C	W	2-1	Yorke 2	22,790
35		18	(a)	Southampton	W	2-1	Hendrie, Yorke	15,238
36		25	(h)	Bolton W	L	1-3	Taylor	38,392
37	May	2	(a)	Sheffield W	W	3-1	Yorke, Hendrie, Joachim	34,177
38		10	(h)	Arsenal	W	1-0	Yorke (pen)	39,372

FINAL LEAGUE POSITION: 7th in the F.A. Premiership

Appearances

Sub. Appearances

Goals

Oakes M	Nelson F	Wright A	Southgate G	Ehiogu U	Townsend A	Taylor I	Draper M	Milosevic S	Collymore S	Yorke D	Grayson S	Joachim J	Charles G	Scimeca R	Bosnich M	Staunton S	Curcic S	Hendrie L	Byfield D	Walker R	Barry G	#
1	2	3	4	5	6	7	8	9	10	11												1
1	2	3	4	5*	7	12	8	9†	10	11	6	13										2
	12	13	4	5		7	8		10	11	9°	14	2	6†	1	3*						3
			4	5*	9	7	8		10	11			2	6	1	3	12					4
	12	3	4	5		7	8		10	11	9		2*		1	6						5
	2	3	4	5		7†	8		10	11	9			12	1	6*	13					6
	2	3	4	5		7	8	12	10*	11		13	14		1	6°	9†					7
	2	3	4	5		7*	8		10	11	9	12			1	6						8
	2†	3	4	5		7	8	12	10	11			13		1	6	9*					9
	2°	3	4	5		7		9*	10	11	8		14	13	1	6†	12					10
	12		4	5		7		9		11	10	13	2	6*	1	3	8†					11
	7	3	4	5			8	9	10	11			2	6	1							12
1	7*	3	4	5		12	8	13	9	10	11†		2	6								13
	2	3	4			7		9		11	8	12	5*	10	1	6						14
1	7	3		5			8	9	10	11			2	4		6						15
1	7	3		5			8	9	10	11	12		2	4*		6						16
		3	4	5			8	9*	10†	11°	7	12	2		1	6	13	14				17
1		3	4			7	8	9*	10	11†		12	2			6	13					18
1		3	4			7	8	9	10	11*			2			6	12					19
	2	3		5		7	8	9	10	11				4	1	6						20
	2	3		5		7	8	9		11				4	1	6		10*	12			21
	2*	3		5		7	8	9	10	11		12		4	1	6						22
	2	3		5		7	8	9	10	11	4				1	6						23
		3*	4	5		7	8		10	9	2	12		6	1			11				24
	12	3	4	5		8			10	9†	2	7		6	1		11*	13				25
	2	3	4	5		7		9	10			8	11	6	1							26
	2†	3	4	5		7		9*	10			8	11	6	1		12	13				27
		3	4	5		7			10*	9	2	11		6	1		8	12				28
		3	4	5		7	8			9	2	11			1	6	10					29
	12	3*	4	5		7	8			9	2†	11			1	6	10	13				30
	2†	3	4	5		7	8*	9			12	11	13		1	6	10					31
		3	4	5		7	8			9	12	11†	2		1	6	10*	13				32
		3	4	5		7	8†	12		9	13	11	2*		1	6	10					33
		3	4	5		7		9*		11	2	8			1	6	10					34
		3	4	5		7	8			9	2*	11	12		1	6	10					35
		3	4*	5		7	8	9†	13	11	12	10	14		1	6°	2					36
1	2	3	4	5		7†	8			9	6	11						10*	12	13		37
	2	3	4	5			8	12		9	6	11*			1		10			7		38
8	21	35	32	37	3	30	31	19	23	30	28	16	14	16	30	27	3	13	1		1	
	4	2			2		4	2		5	10	4	5			4	4	6	1	1		
				2		6	3	7	6	12		8	1			1		3				

77

1998-99

1	Aug	15	(a)	Everton	D	0-0			40,112
2		23	(h)	Middlesbrough	W	3-1	Joachim, Charles, Thompson		29,559
3		29	(a)	Sheffield Wednesd	W	1-0	Joachim		25,989
4	Sep	9	(h)	Newcastle United	W	1-0	Hendrie (pen)		39,241
5		12	(h)	Wimbledon	W	2-0	Merson, Taylor		32,959
6		19	(a)	Leeds United	D	0-0			33,162
7		26	(h)	Derby County	W	1-0	Merson		38,007
8	Oct	3	(a)	Coventry City	W	2-1	Taylor 2		22,650
9		17	(a)	West Ham United	D	0-0			26,002
10		24	(h)	Leicester City	D	1-1	Ehiogu		39,241
11	Nov	7	(h)	Tottenham Hotspur	W	3-2	Dublin 2, Collymore		39,241
12		14	(a)	Southampton	W	4-1	Dublin 3, Merson		15,242
13		21	(h)	Liverpool	L	2-4	Dublin 2		39,241
14		28	(a)	Nottingham Forest	D	2-2	Joachim 2		25,753
15	Dec	5	(h)	Manchester United	D	1-1	Joachim		39,241
16		9	(a)	Chelsea	L	1-2	Hendrie		34,765
17		13	(h)	Arsenal	W	3-2	Joachim, Dublin 2		39,217
18		21	(a)	Charlton Athletic	W	1-0	Rufus (og)		20,043
19		26	(a)	Blackburn Rovers	L	1-2	Scimeca		27,536
20		28	(h)	Sheffield Wednesd	W	2-1	Southgate, Ehiogu		39,217
21	Jan	9	(a)	Middlesbrough	D	0-0			34,643
22		18	(h)	Everton	W	3-0	Joachim 2, Merson		32,488
23		30	(a)	Newcastle United	L	1-2	Merson		36,766
24	Feb	6	(h)	Blackburn Rovers	L	1-3	Joachim		37,404
25		17	(h)	Leeds United	L	1-2	Scimeca		37,510
26		21	(a)	Wimbledon	D	0-0			15,582
27		27	(h)	Coventry City	L	1-4	Dublin (pen)		38,799
28	Mar	10	(a)	Derby County	L	1-2	Thompson		26,836
29		13	(a)	Tottenham Hotspur	L	0-1			35,963
30		21	(h)	Chelsea	L	0-3			39,217
31	Apr	2	(h)	West Ham United	D	0-0			36,813
32		6	(a)	Leicester City	D	2-2	Hendrie, Joachim		20,652
33		10	(h)	Southampton	W	3-0	Draper, Joachim, Dublin		32,203
34		17	(a)	Liverpool	W	1-0	Taylor		44,306
35		24	(h)	Nottingham Forest	W	2-0	Draper, Barry		34,492
36	May	1	(a)	Manchester United	L	1-2	Joachim		55,189
37		8	(h)	Charlton Athletic	L	3-4	Barry, Joachim 2		37,705
38		16	(a)	Arsenal	L	0-1			38,308

FINAL LEAGUE POSITION: 6th in the F.A. Premiership

Appearances

Sub. Appearances

Goals

Bosnich MJ	Charles GA	Wright AG	Southgate G	Scimeca R	Thompson A	Taylor IK	Barry G	Joachim JK	Yorke D	Hendrie LA	Draper MA	Ehiogu U	Grayson SN	Vassell D	Collymore SV	Merson PC	Oakes MC	Watson SC	Dublin D	Rachel A	Stone SB	Calderwood C	Delaney M	
1	2	3	4	5	6*	7	8	9	10	11	12													1
1	2	3	4	9†	6	7	8	10°		11*	14	5	12	13										2
1	2	3	4		11		6	10		7	8*	5	12		9									3
1	2	3	4	9°	11†	12	6	10		7	8*	5	14	13										4
1	2	3	4	13	11°	8†	6	9		7	12	5	14		10*									5
1	2†	3	4		11*	8	6	9		7	13	5	12			10								6
1	2	3	4		11*	8	6†	9°		7	14	5	12		13	10								7
1	2†	3	4		11	8	6	13		7		5	12		9	10*								8
	2	3	4		11	8	6			7		5			9	10	1							9
	2*	3	4		11	8	6	12		7		5			9	10†	1	13						10
		3	4			8	6			7	12	5			11	10	1	2	9*					11
		3	4			8	6	12		7	13	5			11†	10*	1	2	9					12
	12	3†	4	14			6	13		7	8°				11	10	1	2*	9					13
		3	4	12		8	6	7		11		5				10*	1	2	9					14
		3	4			11	8	6	10	7		5					1	2	9					15
		3	4			11	8	6	10*	7		5			12		1	2	9					16
		3	4			11	8	6†	10*	7		5	13		12		1	2	9					17
		3	4	12		6	8			7		5			10*		1	2	9					18
		3	4	6		11	8†	10*		7°		5	14		13		1	2	9	12				19
		3	4	8†		7*	6	10		11	12	5			13		1	2	9					20
		3	4	8*		7	6	10		11		5	12				1	2	9					21
		3	4	8		7°	6	10		11*	14	5			13	12	1	2	9†					22
		3	4	8		7	6	9		11		5*	13	12		10	1	2†						23
		3	4	5		12	8	6*	7						11	10	1	2	9					24
		3	4	5		12	8	6*	7	11					13	10	1	2	9†					25
		3	4	5			8		7*	11			6		12	10	1	2	9					26
		3	4	5			8†	12	7	11	13°		6		14	10	1	2*	9					27
1		3	4	2*	11		6	12		7	8				9	10			5					28
1		3	4	5	11		6	12		7	8				9	10*					2			29
1		3	4	5	11	12	6	14		8*					10†	13		2	9°		7			30
1		3	4		11*	8		10		6						12		2	9		7	5		31
1		3	4		8	12		10		11	6							2*	9		7	5		32
1		3	4		11†	8	13	10		14	6°					12		2	9*		7	5		33
1		3	4		8	13	10*	11†		6						13		2	9		7	5		34
		3	4		8	14		11		6	12					10	1	2†	9*		7°	5	13	35
		3	4		12	8		11		6*					13	10	1	2	9†		7	5		36
		3	4		8	6		9		11†	12				13	10	1	2			7	5*		37
		3	4	8				9		11	5	7*	12			10	1	2°	13		6†	14		38
15	10	38	38	16	20	31	27	29	1	31	13	23	4		11	21	23	26	24		9	8		
1			2	5	2	5	7		1	10	2	11	6	9	5		1			1	1		2	
	1		1	2	2	4	2	14		3	2	2			1	5			11					

79

1999-2000

#	Month	Date		Opponent	Res	Score	Scorers	Attendance
1	Aug	7	(a)	Newcastle United	W	1-0	Joachim	36,376
2		11	(h)	Everton	W	3-0	Joachim, Dublin, Taylor	30,337
3		16	(h)	West Ham United	D	2-2	Dublin 2	26,250
4		21	(a)	Chelsea	L	0-1		35,071
5		24	(a)	Watford	W	1-0	Delaney	19,161
6		28	(h)	Middlesbrough	W	1-0	Dublin	28,728
7	Sep	11	(a)	Arsenal	L	1-3	Joachim	38,093
8		18	(h)	Bradford City	W	1-0	Dublin	28,083
9		25	(a)	Leicester City	L	1-3	Dublin	19,917
10	Oct	2	(h)	Liverpool	D	0-0		39,217
11		18	(a)	Sunderland	L	1-2	Dublin	39,866
12		23	(h)	Wimbledon	D	1-1	Dublin	27,160
13		30	(a)	Manchester United	L	0-3		55,211
14	Nov	6	(h)	Southampton	L	0-1		26,474
15		22	(a)	Coventry City	L	1-2	Dublin	20,174
16		27	(a)	Everton	D	0-0		34,750
17	Dec	4	(h)	Newcastle United	L	0-1		34,531
18		18	(h)	Sheffield Wednesd	W	2-1	Merson, Taylor	23,885
19		26	(a)	Derby County	W	2-0	Boateng, Taylor	33,222
20		29	(h)	Tottenham Hotspur	D	1-1	Taylor	39,217
21	Jan	3	(a)	Leeds United	W	2-1	Southgate 2	40,027
22		15	(a)	West Ham United	D	1-1	Taylor	24,237
23		22	(h)	Chelsea	D	0-0		33,704
24	Feb	5	(h)	Watford	W	4-0	Stone, Merson 2, Walker	27,647
25		14	(a)	Middlesbrough	W	4-0	Carbone, Summerbell (og), Joachim 2	31,591
26		26	(a)	Bradford City	D	1-1	Merson	18,276
27	Mar	5	(h)	Arsenal	D	1-1	Walker	36,930
28		11	(h)	Coventry City	W	1-0	Ehiogu	33,177
29		15	(a)	Liverpool	D	0-0		43,615
30		18	(a)	Southampton	L	0-2		15,218
31		25	(h)	Derby County	W	2-0	Carbone, Boateng	28,613
32	Apr	5	(a)	Sheffield Wednesd	W	1-0	Thompson	18,136
33		9	(h)	Leeds United	W	1-0	Joachim	33,889
34		15	(a)	Tottenham Hotspur	W	4-2	Dublin 2 (1 pen), Carbone, Wright	35,304
35		22	(h)	Leicester City	D	2-2	Thompson, Merson	31,229
36		29	(h)	Sunderland	D	1-1	Barry	33,949
37	May	6	(a)	Wimbledon	D	2-2	Hendrie, Dublin	19,188
38		14	(h)	Manchester United	L	0-1		39,217

FINAL LEAGUE POSITION: 6th in the F.A. Premiership

Appearances

Sub. Appearances

Goals

James DB	Delaney MA	Wright AG	Southgate G	Ehiogu U	Calderwood C	Boateng G	Taylor IK	Dublin D	Joachim JK	Thompson A	Stone SB	Hendrie LA	Merson PC	Draper M	Vassell D	Enckelman P	Watson SC	Barry G	Carbone B	Ghrayib N	Samuel JL	Walker RM	Cutler N	Brewers J	
1	2	3	4	5	6*	7†	8	9	10	11	12	13													1
1	2	3	4	5	6	7*	8	9°	10	11†	14	12	13												2
1	2	3	4	5	6	7*	8	9	10	11†	13	12													3
1	2	3	4	5	6†		8	9	10	11*	12°	7	13	14											4
1	2	3	4	5	6	12	8	9	11			7	10*												5
1	2	3	4	5*	6	12	8	9	11†			7	10	13											6
1*	2	3	4	5	6		8	9°	11	13		7†	10	14	12										7
			4	5		7*	8	9	10°	3†	13	11	12	14		1	2	6							8
	12		4	5	13	7	8	9	10	3†		11				1	2*	6							9
	2		4	5		7†	8	9	10	3	13	11*	12			1		6							10
1	2		4	5		7*	8	9		3	12	11	13	10†				6							11
1	2		4	5		7*	8	9		3†		11	13					6	10	12					12
1	2	12	4	5		7†	8	9		3*	13	11	14					6	10°						13
1	2	3	4	5	13			9	11*			7	10†					6	8	12					14
1	2*	3	4	5	6		8	9	10			7†	11	13	12										15
1		3	4	5		7	8	9	10*			11					2	6	12						16
1	2	3	4	5		7	8	9°	10	13†		11*	14					6	12						17
1		3*	4	5	13	7	8	9†	12				10	14			2	6	11°						18
1		3	4	5		7	8		11	13			10*	12			2	6	9†						19
1		3†	4	5		7	8		11	12			10	13			2	6	9*						20
1		3	4	5			8	11		7			10	12			2	6	9*						21
1		3	4	5	12	7*	8	11		2			10	13				6	9†						22
1	12	3	4	5		7	8	11†		14			10	13°			2*	6	9						23
1	2	3	5	4	8†			11°		7		13	10*					6	9		12	14			24
1*	2	3	4	5	8°	13		11		7		14	10†					6	9		12				25
	2	3	4	5	8	12		11		7*		13	10†			1		6	9						26
	2	3	4	5	8			11		7	12		10			1		6	9*						27
	2	3	4	5		7	8	11†		12			10*			1		6	9	13					28
	2	3	4*	5	8	12		11°		7		13	10†			1		6	9	14					29
	3*		5	4		8		13	12	7†		11°	10			1	2	6	9		14				30
1	2	3	5			7	8†	13	11°	14	12		10					6	9*	4					31
1	2†	3°	5					9	14	11	12	8					7	6			13	4	10*		32
1		3°	5			7			14	11	13	8†	10				2	6	9*		12	4			33
1	12†	3	5			7		9		11			10				2*	6	8	4			13		34
1		3		5		7		9*	12	11†		13	10				2	6	8		4				35
1	2		4	5		7		13	9*	11†	14		10					6	8	3°	12				36
1	2	3†	4	5					9*	11	13	7	10					6	8		12				37
	2	3	4	5		7°	14	9	13	12		11*	10			1		6	8†						38
29	25	31	31	31	15	30	25	23	27	16	10	18	24		1	9	13	30	22	1	5	2			
3	1			3	3	4	3	6	5	14	11	8	1	10	1	1		2	4	4	3	1	1		
1	1	2	1		2	5	12	6	2	1	1	5						1	3		2				

2000-2001

1	Aug	19	(a)	Leicester City	D	0-0		21,455
2		27	(h)	Chelsea	D	1-1	Nilis	27,056
3	Sep	6	(a)	Liverpool	L	1-3	Stone	43,360
4		9	(a)	Ipswich Town	W	2-1	Hendrie, Dublin	22,064
5		16	(h)	Bradford City	W	2-0	Southgate, Dublin (pen)	27,849
6		23	(a)	Middlesbrough	D	1-1	Joachim	27,556
7		30	(h)	Derby County	W	4-1	Joachim 2, Merson, Wright	27,941
8	Oct	14	(a)	Arsenal	L	0-1		38,046
9		22	(h)	Sunderland	D	0-0		27,215
10		28	(h)	Charlton Athletic	W	2-1	Taylor, Merson	27,461
11	Nov	5	(a)	Everton	W	1-0	Merson	27,670
12		11	(h)	Tottenham Hotspur	W	2-0	Taylor 2	33,608
13		18	(a)	Southampton	L	0-2		14,979
14		25	(a)	Coventry City	D	1-1	Dublin	21,455
15	Dec	2	(h)	Newcastle United	D	1-1	Dublin	34,255
16		9	(a)	West Ham United	D	1-1	Hendrie	25,888
17		16	(h)	Manchester City	D	2-2	Dublin, Ginola	29,281
18		23	(a)	Leeds United	W	2-1	Southgate, Boateng	39,714
19		26	(h)	Manchester United	L	0-1		40,889
20	Jan	1	(a)	Chelsea	L	0-1		33,159
21		13	(h)	Liverpool	L	0-3		41,366
22		20	(a)	Manchester United	L	0-2		67,533
23		24	(h)	Leeds United	L	1-2	Merson	29,335
24	Feb	3	(a)	Bradford City	W	3-0	Vassell 2, Joachim	19,591
25		10	(h)	Middlesbrough	D	1-1	Stone	28,912
26		24	(a)	Derby County	L	0-1		27,289
27	Mar	5	(a)	Sunderland	D	1-1	Joachim	44,114
28		10	(h)	Ipswich Town	W	2-1	Joachim 2	28,216
29		18	(h)	Arsenal	D	0-0		36,111
30		31	(a)	Manchester City	W	3-1	Merson, Dublin, Hendrie	34,243
31	Apr	4	(h)	Leicester City	W	2-1	Dublin, Hendrie	29,043
32		7	(h)	West Ham United	D	2-2	Ginola, Hendrie	31,432
33		14	(h)	Everton	W	2-1	Dublin, Taylor	31,272
34		17	(a)	Charlton Athletic	D	3-3	Ginola, Vassell, Hendrie	20,043
35		21	(h)	Southampton	D	0-0		29,336
36		28	(a)	Tottenham Hotspur	D	0-0		36,096
37	May	5	(h)	Coventry City	W	3-2	Vassell, Angel, Merson	39,761
38		19	(a)	Newcastle United	L	0-3		51,306

FINAL LEAGUE POSITION: 8th in the F.A. Premiership

Appearances

Sub. Appearances

Goals

James DB	Stone SB	Wright AG	Southgate G	Alpay	Barry G	Hendrie LA	Boateng G	Dublin D	Merson PC	Ginola DDM	Vassell D	Nilis L	Taylor IK	Joachim JK	Ehiogu U	De Bilde GRG	Delaney MA	Samuel JL	Staunton S	McGrath J	Hitzlsperger T	Angel JPA	No.
1	2	3	4	5	6	7	8	9	10	11*	12												1
1	2	3	4	5	6	7*	11	9	10			8†	12	13									2
1	2		4	6*	3	13	11†	9	10	12		8	7			5							3
1	2	3	4*	5	6	7	11	9	10	14	13°	8†				12							4
1	2	3	4	5	6	7*	8	9	10	11†			12	13									5
1	2	3	4	5	6	12	8*	9	10	11†			7	13									6
1	2	3	4	5	6	8*	12	9	10	11†	14		7	13°									7
1	2	3†	4	5	6	11	13	9*	10			12	7	8									8
1	2	3	4	5	6	11*	13	9†	10			12	7	8									9
1	2	3	4	5	6		11	9	10			12	7	8*									10
1	2†	3	4	5	6		11		10		13		7	8		9*	12						11
1	2	3	4†	5	6		11	9	10		13		7	8*			12						12
1	2°	3	4	5	6*	14	11	9	10†		13		7	8			12						13
1	2	3	4	5	6	8	11	9	10				7*				12						14
1	2	3	4	5	6	7	8	9	10	11*									12				15
1	2	3	4	5	6	7	8	9	10	11													16
1	2	3	4	5	6*	7	8	9	10	11							12						17
1	2	3	4	5	6	7	8		10	11†	12					9*		13					18
1	2	3	4	5°	6†	7	8	14	10	11	13					9*	12						19
1	7	3	4				11	9*	10		13		6			8	2		5†	12			20
1	2	3	4	5*	8			9	10	11†	14					7°	6	12	13				21
1	2	3		5	4*	7	11	9	10	12	13								6			8†	22
1	2°	3*		5	4	8	11		10	13	14		7†				12		6			9	23
1		3		5	4*	7	11		10°			8	12	13			2		6	14		9†	24
1	7	3		5		11†	4	12	10		13	8					2		6			9*	25
1	2	3*		5	4	12	11†	9	10	13			7	14					6			8°	26
1	2	3		5	4	11		9	10				7	8					6				27
1	2		4	5	12	7		9	10	11*			6	8					3				28
1	2	3	4	5		7		12	10	11	13		6	8*								9†	29
1	7	3	4	5		8	11	9*	10†		13		6°	14			2		12				30
1	7*	3	4	5		8	11†	9	10	12			6	13			2						31
1	7†	12	4		5	8			10	11	13		6	9			2		3*				32
1	7†	3	4	5		8*	11	9°	10	13	12		6				2					14	33
1	7†	3		5		8	11*	9	10	12	13		4				2		6				34
1		3	4		5	7	11	9	10		8		6*				2						35
1		3	4		5		11	9	10	12	8†		7	13			2		6*				36
1		3	4		5	14	11*	9	10	12	8°		7				2		6†			13	37
1	13	3	4	5		7	14	12	10	11†	8°		6				2					9*	38
38	33	35	31	33	29	27	29	29	38	14	5	3	25	11	1	4	12	1	13			7	
	1	1			1	5	4	4		13	18	4	9	1		7	2	1	3	1	2		
	2	1	2			6	1	8	6	3	4	1	4	7								1	

2001-2002

1	Aug	18	(a)	Tottenham Hotspur	D	0-0		36,059
2		26	(h)	Manchester United	D	1-1	Vassell	42,632
3	Sep	8	(a)	Liverpool	W	3-1	Dublin, Hendrie, Vassell	44,102
4		16	(h)	Sunderland	D	0-0		31,688
5		24	(a)	Southampton	W	3-1	Boateng, Angel, Hadji	26,794
6		30	(h)	Blackburn Rovers	W	2-0	Angel, Vassell	28,623
7	Oct	14	(h)	Fulham	W	2-0	Vassell, Taylor	28,579
8		20	(a)	Everton	L	2-3	Hadji, Schmeichel	33,352
9		24	(h)	Charlton Athletic	W	1-0	Kachloul	27,701
10		27	(h)	Bolton Wanderers	W	3-2	Angel 2 (1 pen), Vassell	33,599
11	Nov	3	(a)	Newcastle United	L	0-3		51,057
12		17	(h)	Middlesbrough	D	0-0		35,424
13		25	(a)	Leeds United	D	1-1	Kachloul	40,159
14	Dec	1	(h)	Leicester City	L	0-2		30,711
15		5	(a)	West Ham United	D	1-1	Dublin	28,377
16		9	(a)	Arsenal	L	2-3	Merson, Stone	38,074
17		17	(h)	Ipswich Town	W	2-1	Angel 2	29,320
18		22	(a)	Derby County	L	1-3	Angel	28,001
19		26	(h)	Liverpool	L	1-2	Hendrie	42,602
20		29	(h)	Tottenham Hotspur	D	1-1	Angel (pen)	41,134
21	Jan	1	(a)	Sunderland	D	1-1	Taylor	45,324
22		12	(h)	Derby County	W	2-1	Vassell, Angel	28,881
23		21	(a)	Charlton Athletic	W	2-1	Vassell, Angel	25,681
24		30	(h)	Everton	D	0-0		32,460
25	Feb	2	(a)	Fulham	D	0-0		20,041
26		9	(h)	Chelsea	D	1-1	Merson	41,137
27		23	(a)	Manchester United	L	0-1		67,592
28	Mar	2	(h)	West Ham United	W	2-1	Angel, Vassell	37,341
29		5	(a)	Blackburn Rovers	L	0-3		21,988
30		17	(h)	Arsenal	L	1-2	Dublin	41,520
31		23	(a)	Ipswich Town	D	0-0		25,247
32		30	(a)	Bolton Wanderers	L	2-3	Warhurst (og), Taylor	24,600
33	Apr	2	(h)	Newcastle United	D	1-1	Crouch	36,597
34		6	(a)	Middlesbrough	L	1-2	Angel	26,003
35		13	(h)	Leeds United	L	0-1		40,039
36		20	(a)	Leicester City	D	2-2	Vassell, Hitzlsperger	18,125
37		27	(h)	Southampton	W	2-1	Vassell 2	35,255
38	May	11	(a)	Chelsea	W	3-1	Crouch, Vassell, Dublin	40,709

FINAL LEAGUE POSITION: 8th in the F.A. Premiership

Appearances

Sub. Appearances

Goals

Schmeichel PB	Delaney MA	Wright AG	Mellberg EO	Aplay	Boateng G	Kachloul H	Vassell D	Angel JPA	Merson PC	Hendrie LA	Stone SB	Hadji M	Ginola D	Balaban B	Dublin D	Staunton S	Samuel JL	Taylor IK	Enckelman P	Barry G	Hitzlsperger T	Crouch PJ	
1	2	3	4	5	6	7°	8†	9*	10	11	12	13	14										1
1	2	3	4	5	6	7	8	9†	10*	11		13		12									2
1	2	3	4	5	6	7	8		10*	11†		12				9	13						3
1	2	3	4	5	6	7	8		10*	11		13	12			9†							4
1	2	3	4	5	6	7†		8°		11*	14	10			13	9	12						5
1	2	3		5	6	7†	8	9*		11		10				13	4	12					6
1		3		5	6	7†	8	9*		11	2	10				13	4	12					7
1	2	3	5°	6		8	9†		11*		10	14				13	4	12	7				8
1	2	3		5	6	7	8		11*		10					9	4	12					9
1	2	3		5	6	7	8*	9†	12	11°		10				13	4	14					10
1	2	3		5	6	7	8	9*		11†		10				12	4	13					11
1	2†	3	4	5	6	11*	8	9		10	7		13				12						12
1		3	4	5	6	7	8	9*	10	11†	2					12		13					13
1	2	3	4	5°	6		8†	9	10	11*	7		14			13	12						14
	2†	3	4		6		13		10*	8	7					9	5	12	1	11			15
		3	4		6		12		10	8	7					9	5	2	1	11*			16
1		3	4		6		13	9*	10	8†	7					12	5	2		11			17
1		3	4		6°	12		8	10	14	7				13	9	5	2†		11*			18
1		3	4		6	7	8	9	10	11†	12					5	2*	13					19
1		3*	4		6†	7	8	9	10	11	12					5	2	13					20
1		3	4			11*	8		10	7						9	5	2	6	12			21
1	2		4		6	12	8	9	10°	11†		14				5	3	7*		13			22
1	2		4		6		8	9	10	11*		7				5	3			12			23
	2		4		6	12	8†	9	10	11*		7			13	5	3		1				24
	2		4		6	12	8	9*	10	11†	13	7				5	3		1				25
	2	4°		6		8*	9	10	11†	14	7				13	5	3		1	12			26
1	2		4		6		8	9		7	10†					12	5	3*		11	13		27
1	2		4		6		8	9	12	7*						5	3			11	10		28
1	2		4		6		8	9°	12	14	7*	13				5	3			11	10†		29
1	2		4		6	7°		9†	10*	14	12				13	5	3			11	8		30
1	2		4		6		8	9		7						5	3*	12		11	10		31
1	2†		4		6		8*	13		7						5	12	11		3	10	9	32
1	2		4		6†		13	8	12	7*		14				5	11			3	10	9°	33
1	2		4		6		12	8		7*						5	11			3	10	9	34
	2		4		6†	7°	14	8*		12						5	13	11	1	3	10	9	35
	2		4		6		12	8†		7		13				5	3*		1	11	10	9	36
	2	3	4		6		8	13		7†	12					5	14		1	11°	10	9	37
	2	3	4		6	8°		13	14	7		12				5			1	11	10*	9†	38
29	30	23	32	14	37	17	30	26	18	25	14	17			9	30	17	7	9	16	11	7	
				5	6	3	3	4	8	6	5	8			12	3	6	9		4	1		
1				1	2	12	12	2	2	1	2				4		3			1	2		

2002-2003

1	Aug	18	(h)	Liverpool	L	0-1		41,183
2		24	(a)	Tottenham Hotspur	L	0-1		35,384
3		28	(h)	Manchester City	W	1-0	Vassell	33,494
4	Sep	1	(a)	Bolton Wanderers	L	0-1		22,500
5		11	(h)	Charlton Athletic	W	2-0	De La Cruz, Moore	26,483
6		16	(a)	Birmingham City	L	0-3		29,505
7		22	(h)	Everton	W	3-2	Hendrie 2, Dublin	30,023
8		28	(a)	Sunderland	L	0-1		40,492
9	Oct	6	(h)	Leeds United	D	0-0		33,505
10		21	(h)	Southampton	L	0-1		25,817
11		26	(a)	Manchester United	D	1-1	Mellberg	67,619
12	Nov	3	(a)	Blackburn Rovers	D	0-0		23,004
13		9	(h)	Fulham	W	3-1	Angel, Allback, Leonhardsen	29,563
14		16	(a)	West Bromwich Alb	D	0-0		27,091
15		23	(h)	West Ham United	W	4-1	Hendrie, Leonhardsen, Dublin, Vassell	33,279
16		30	(a)	Arsenal	L	1-3	Hitzlsperger	38,090
17	Dec	7	(h)	Newcastle United	L	0-1		33,446
18		14	(h)	West Bromwich Alb	W	2-1	Vassell, Hitzlsperger	40,391
19		21	(a)	Chelsea	L	0-2		38,284
20		26	(a)	Manchester City	L	1-3	Dublin	33,991
21		28	(h)	Middlesbrough	W	1-0	Dublin	33,637
22	Jan	1	(h)	Bolton Wanderers	W	2-0	Dublin, Vassell	31,838
23		11	(a)	Liverpool	D	1-1	Dublin (pen)	43,210
24		18	(h)	Tottenham Hotspur	L	0-1		38,576
25		28	(a)	Middlesbrough	W	5-2	Vassell 2, Gudjonsson, Barry, Dublin	27,546
26	Feb	2	(h)	Blackburn Rovers	W	3-0	Dublin 2, Barry	29,171
27		8	(a)	Fulham	L	1-2	Barry	17,092
28		22	(a)	Charlton Athletic	L	0-3		26,257
29	Mar	3	(h)	Birmingham City	L	0-2		42,602
30		15	(h)	Manchester United	L	0-1		42,602
31		22	(a)	Southampton	D	2-2	Hendrie, Vassell	31,888
32	Apr	5	(h)	Arsenal	D	1-1	Toure (og)	42,602
33		12	(a)	West Ham United	D	2-2	Vassell (pen), Leonhardsen	35,029
34		19	(h)	Chelsea	W	2-1	Allback 2	39,358
35		21	(a)	Newcastle United	D	1-1	Dublin	52,015
36		26	(a)	Everton	L	1-2	Allback	40,167
37	May	3	(h)	Sunderland	W	1-0	Allback	36,963
38		11	(a)	Leeds United	L	1-3	Gudjonsson	40,205

FINAL LEAGUE POSITION: 16th in the F.A. Premiership

Appearances

Sub. Appearances

Goals

Enckelman P	Delaney MA	Barry G	Mellberg EO	Alpay	Staunton S	De La Cruz BU	Vassell D	Crouch PJ	Hitzlsperger T	Hendrie LA	Samuel JL	Allback M	Hadji M	Wright AG	Kinsella MA	Angel JPA	Johnsen JR	Moore S	Dublin D	Leonhardsen O	Postma S	Taylor IK	Edwards RO	Cooke S	Gudjonsson JK	Whittingham P	
1	2	3*	4	5	6	7	8	9°	10†	11	12	13	14														1
1	2	6*	4		5	7†	8	9°		11	12	14		3	10	13											2
1	2	6	4		5		7	9		11	12	13		3*	10	8†											3
1	2	6	4		5	13	7*	9†		11	12	14		3°	10	8											4
1		11	4	5	3	2		13			7	8†			10	9*	6	12									5
1		11	4	5	3	2	12				7	8†			10	9*	6		13								6
1		11	4		5	2°	8†	9*		7	3				10		6	14	13	12							7
1	2*	11	4		5	12	8	13		7	3					10°	6		9†	14							8
1		11	4		5	2	8			7	3					10	13	6*	9	12†							9
1		11	4	5	6	2*	8			7†	3	12				10°	13		9	14							10
1	2	11	4		5			14		12	3				10	13	8°		9†	7*		6					11
1	2	11	4		5			13			3				10	8†	12		9*	7		6					12
1	2	11	4		5°			14			3	13			10*	8†	12		9	7		6					13
1	2	11	4		13			14	10	12	3°	8†					5*		9	7		6					14
1		3	4		5		8†		10	11*	2	12			14	13			9°	7		6					15
1		2	4		5	12	8		10	11*	3								9	7		6					16
1		6*	4			2	8		10	11	3				12	13	5		9†	7							17
1		3	4		6		8		10	11	2						5		9	7							18
1		3	4		5		8†		10	11	2	13	6		14	12			9°	7*							19
1		3	4		5	7	8°		10*	14	2				11		6	12	9	13†							20
		11	4			13†			10		2	14	7*	12	6	8	5°		9		1		3				21
		11	4		7°			13	10†	6	5			3	14	8*			9		1		2		12		22
1		11	4			12	8†		10	7*	2			3			5	13	9			6					23
1	2	11	4			12	13	14	10	7*	3						5	8°	9†			6					24
1	2	11	4			13	8		10	12	3						5	7*	9						6†		25
1	2*	11	4			12	8	14	10		3					13	5	7†	9						6°		26
1		11	4			13	8	14	10†	12	3						5	7*	9			2°			6		27
1		11	4		5	2*	8†	9		13		14		12	3°	10	6					7					28
1		11	4				8	13		6	2			12	3*		5	7†	9						10		29
		11	4				8		10	6	2	7			3		5		9*		1				12		30
		11	4				8	9*	10	6†	2	13	7		3		5	12			1						31
1		6	4		2°		9		10	7	3	14	8†				5		13				12		11*		32
1		6	4		5		8		10	7°	3	9†	11*		14				13			2	12				33
1		6	4			12	8		10		3	9					5					7		2	11*		34
1		11°	4		6		8		10*		3	9					5		13	7			12	2†		14	35
1			4		6	14	8		10		3						5†		9	7*			13	2°	11	12	36
1			4		3		8		10°	11*	2	9					5	14		7†		6	12	13			37
		3	4				8		10		2†	9					5*	7°	13		1		12	14	6	11	38
33	12	35	38	5	22	12	28	7	24	22	33	9	7	9	15	8	25	7	23	13	5	9	7		9	1	
					4	8	5	7	2	5	5	11	4	1	4	7	1	6	5	6	1	4	1	3	2	3	
		3	1		1	8		2	4		5					1	1		10	3					2		

87

2003-2004

1	Aug	16	(a)	Portsmouth	L	1-2	Barry (pen)	20,101
2		24	(h)	Liverpool	D	0-0		42,573
3		27	(a)	Arsenal	L	0-2		38,010
4		30	(h)	Leicester City	W	3-1	Angel 2, Thatcher (og)	32,274
5	Sep	14	(a)	Manchester City	L	1-4	Angel	46,687
6		20	(h)	Charlton Athletic	W	2-1	Alpay, Samuel	31,410
7		27	(a)	Chelsea	L	0-1		41,182
8	Oct	5	(h)	Bolton Wanderers	D	1-1	Angel	30,229
9		19	(a)	Birmingham City	D	0-0		29,546
10		25	(h)	Everton	D	0-0		36,146
11	Nov	1	(a)	Newcastle United	D	1-1	Dublin	51,975
12		8	(h)	Middlesbrough	L	0-2		29,898
13		23	(a)	Tottenham Hotspur	L	1-2	Allback	33,140
14		29	(h)	Southampton	W	1-0	Dublin	31,285
15	Dec	6	(a)	Manchester United	L	0-4		67,621
16		14	(h)	Wolves	W	3-2	Angel 2, Barry	36,964
17		20	(a)	Blackburn Rovers	W	2-0	S Moore, Angel	20,722
18		26	(a)	Leeds United	D	0-0		38,513
19		28	(h)	Fulham	W	3-0	Vassell 2, Angel	35,617
20	Jan	6	(h)	Portsmouth	W	2-1	Angel, Vassell	28,625
21		10	(a)	Liverpool	L	0-1		43,771
22		18	(h)	Arsenal	L	0-2		39,380
23		31	(a)	Leicester City	W	5-0	Vassell 2, Crouch 2, Dublin	31,056
24	Feb	7	(h)	Leeds United	W	2-0	Angel (pen), Johnsen	39,171
25		11	(a)	Fulham	W	2-1	Angel, Vassell	16,153
26		22	(h)	Birmingham City	D	2-2	Vassell, Hitzlsperger	40,061
27		28	(a)	Everton	L	0-2		39,353
28	Mar	14	(a)	Wolves	W	4-0	Hitzlsperger, Mellberg, Angel 2	29,386
29		20	(h)	Blackburn Rovers	L	0-2		37,532
30		27	(a)	Charlton Athletic	W	2-1	Vassell, Samuel	26,250
31	Apr	4	(h)	Manchester City	D	1-1	Angel	37,602
32		10	(a)	Bolton Wanderers	D	2-2	Crouch, Hendrie	26,374
33		12	(h)	Chelsea	W	3-2	Vassell (pen), Hitzlsperger, Hendrie	41,112
34		18	(h)	Newcastle United	D	0-0		40,786
35		24	(a)	Middlesbrough	W	2-1	Barry, Crouch	31,322
36	May	2	(h)	Tottenham Hotspur	W	1-0	Angel	42,573
37		8	(a)	Southampton	D	1-1	Angel (pen)	32,054
38		15	(h)	Manchester United	L	0-2		42,573

FINAL LEAGUE POSITION: 6th in the F.A. Premiership

Appearances

Sub. Appearances

Goals

Sorensen T	Delaney MA	Samuel JL	Johnsen JR	Alpay	Barry G	McCann GP	Allback M	Angel JPA	Hendrie LA	Whittingham P	Crouch PJ	Hitzlsperger T	Mellberg EO	Vassell D	Dublin D	De La Cruz BU	Kinsella MA	Hadji M	Postma S	Moore S	Ridgewell L	Solano NA	Moore L	
1	2	3	4	5	6	7	8	9*	10	11†	12	13												1
1	2	3	5		6	7		9*	10†	11			4	8	12	13								2
1	2	3	5		6			9	10	11			4	12	7	8*								3
1	2	3	5*	12	6			9	7†	11	10		4	8°	14	13								4
1	2	3	5†	12	6	8		9°	7	11	10		4*	14			13							5
1	4	3		5	6	7	8*	9	10	11				12		2								6
1	2	3		5	6	8		9	10	11*				12	4	7								7
1*	2	3		5	6	7	13	9	10	11†			4	8						12				8
1	2	3	5		6	11		9	10*	12			4	8		7								9
1	2	3			6*	7		9		11		13	4	8	5	12	10†							10
1	2	3	5		6	8	13	9†		11	10		4	7*						12				11
1	2	3	5		6*	7	8†	9	10°	11	12		4	14	13									12
1	2*	3	5		6	9			7†	11	10		4	8	12					13				13
1		3			6	7	12	9*	10†	11°		14	4	8	5	2				13				14
1	2	3			6	7	12	9*	10	11†		13	4	8	5									15
1*	2	3			6	11	8†	9					10	4	7	5	13			12				16
1	2	3			6*	7		9	10°	11		12	4	13	5	14		8†						17
1	2	3			6	7		9	10†	11		12	4	13	5			8*						18
1	2*	3	5		6	7		9†	10°	11		14	4	8						13	12			19
1	2	3			6	7		9†	10	11°	13	14	4	8*	5					12				20
1	2	3	14		6	7*		9	10°	11	12		4	8†	5					13				21
1	2	3	5		6*		8°	9	7†	11	14	10	4			13				12				22
1	2*	3			6	11	13			14	9	10°	4	8†	5	12						7		23
1		3	12		6			9	10°			13	11	4	8†	5*	2			14	7			24
1	2*	3	5		6†			9	10°	13			11	4	8	12				14	7			25
1		3	5*		6†			9	10°	13		11	4	8	12	2					7	14		26
1		3	5		6			9	10		12	11	4	8*		2					7			27
1		3	5		6			9†	10°	14	13	11	4	8		2					7	12		28
1		3			6*			9	10	14	12	11	4	8°		2				5	7†	13		29
1		3	5		6*	7		9	10			11	4	8†		2				12		13		30
1		3	5		6	7		9†	10		13	11	4	8*		2						12		31
1		3			6	7			10°	14	9†	11	4	8*	13	2				5		12		32
1		3	5		6	7			10°	14	9†	11	4	8*	12	2						13		33
1		3	5*		6		14		10	13	9°	11	4	8		2				12	7†			34
1	13	3	5		6*	10		9°			12	14	11	4	8†		2			5	7			35
1	12	3			6	10	14	9°			8†	11	4		13	2				5	7			36
1		3	5		6	7		9†	10°	14	12	11		8*	13	2				4				37
1		3			6*	7	13	9	10°	14	8†	11	4		12	2				5				38
38	23	38	21	4	36	28	7	33	32	20	6	22	33	26	12	20	2		2	5	10			
	2		2	2			8		12	10	10		6	11	8	1	2	6	6			7		
		2	1	1	3		1	16	2		4	3	1	9	3					1				

F.A. CUP COMPETITION

1974/75 SEASON
3rd Round
Jan 4 vs Oldham Athletic (a) 3-0
Att: 14,510 Little B, Nicholl, Graydon

4th Round
Jan 25 vs Sheffield United (h) 4-1
Att: 35,881 Leonard 2, Nicholl, Graydon

5th Round
Feb 15 vs Ipswich Town (a) 2-3
Att: 31,297 McDonald, Evans

1975/76 SEASON
3rd Round
Jan 3 vs Southampton (a) 1-1
Att: 24,138 Gray

Replay
Jan 7 vs Southampton (h) 1-2 (aet.)
Att: 44,623 Graydon

1976/77 SEASON
3rd Round
Jan 8 vs Leicester City (a) 1-0
Att: 27,112 Gray

4th Round
Jan 29 vs West Ham United (h) 3-0
Att: 46,954 Mortimer, Deehan 2

5th Round
Feb 26 vs Port Vale (h) 3-0
Att: 48,812 Nicholl, Deehan, Little

6th Round
Mar 19 vs Manchester United (a) 1-2
Att: 57,089 Little

1977/78 SEASON
3rd Round
Jan 7 vs Everton (a) 1-4
Att: 46,320 Gray

1978/79 SEASON
3rd Round
Jan 6 vs Nottingham Forest (a) 0-2
Att: 29,550

1979/80 SEASON
3rd Round
Jan 4 vs Bristol Rovers (a) 2-1
Att: 16,060 Cowans, Shaw

4th Round
Jan 26 vs Cambridge United (a) 1-1
Att: 12,000 Donovan

Replay
Jan 30 vs Cambridge United (h) 4-1
Att: 36,835 Evans A, Little, Donovan 2

5th Round
Feb 16 vs Blackburn Rovers (a) 1-1
Att: 29,468 Geddis

Replay
Feb 20 vs Blackburn Rovers (h) 1-0
Att: 42,161 Evans A

6th Round
Mar 8 vs West Ham United (a) 0-1
Att: 36,393

1980/81 SEASON
3rd Round
Jan 3 vs Ipswich Town (h) 0-1
Att: 27,721

1981/82 SEASON
3rd Round
Jan 5 vs Notts County (a) 6-0
Att: 12,312 Richards (og), Shaw, Geddis 3,

Cowans (pen)

4th Round
Jan 23 vs Bristol City (a) 1-0
Att: 20,279 Shaw

5th Round
Feb 13 vs Tottenham Hotspur (a) 0-1
Att: 42,950

1982/83 SEASON
3rd Round
Jan 8 vs Northampton Town (a) 1-0
Att: 14,529 Walters

4th Round
Jan 29 vs Wolverhampton Wands. (h) 1-0
Att: 43,121 Withe

5th Round
Feb 19 vs Watford (h) 4-1
Att: 34,330 Shaw, Morley, Gibson, Cowans

6th Round
Mar 12 vs Arsenal (a) 0-2
Att: 41,774

1983/84 SEASON
3rd Round
Jan 7 vs Norwich City (h) 1-1
Att: 21,454 Withe

Replay
Jan 11 vs Norwich City (a) 0-3
Att: 16,420

1984/85 SEASON
3rd Round
Jan 5 vs Liverpool (a) 0-3
Att: 36,877

1985/86 SEASON
3rd Round
Jan 4 vs Portsmouth (a) 2-2
Att: 17,732 Birch, Kerr

Replay
Jan 13 vs Portsmouth (h) 3-2
Att: 14,958 Stainrod 2, Evans

4th Round
Jan 25 vs Millwall (h) 1-1
Att: 12,205 Hodge

Replay
Jan 29 vs Millwall (a) 0-1
Att: 10,273

1986/87 SEASON
3rd Round
Jan 10 vs Chelsea (h) 2-2
Att: 21,997 Cooper, Hunt

Replay
Jan 21 vs Chelsea (a) 1-2
Att: 13,473 Hunt

1987/88 SEASON
3rd Round
Jan 9 vs Leeds United (a) 2-1
Att: 29,002 Gray A, McInally

4th Round
Jan 31 vs Liverpool (h) 0-2
Att: 46,324

1988/89 SEASON
3rd Round
Jan 7 vs Crewe Alexandra (a) 3-2
Att: 5,500 Platt, Gage, McInally

4th Round
Jan 28 vs Wimbledon (h) 0-1
Att: 25,043

1989/90 SEASON
3rd Round
Jan 6 vs Blackburn Rovers (a) 2-2
Att: 14,456 Olney, Ormondroyd

Replay
Jan 10 vs Blackburn Rovers (h) 3-1
Att: 31,169 Ormondroyd, Daley, May (og)

4th Round
Jan 27 vs Port Vale (h) 6-0
Att: 36,532 Platt, Birch 2, Olney, Gray 2

5th Round
Feb 17 vs West Bromwich Albion (a) 2-0
Att: 26,585 Mountfield, Daley

6th Round
Mar 14 vs Oldham Athletic (a) 0-3
Att: 19,490

1990/91 SEASON
3rd Round
Jan 5 vs Wimbledon (h) 1-1
Att: 19,305 Gray

Replay
Jan 9 vs Wimbledon (a) 0-1
Att: 7,382

1991/92 SEASON
3rd Round
Jan 5 vs Tottenham Hotspur (h) 0-0
Att: 29,316

Replay
Jan 14 vs Tottenham Hotspur (a) 1-0
Att: 25,462 Yorke

4th Round
Feb 5 vs Derby County (a) 4-3
Att: 22,452 Yorke 3, Parker

5th Round
Feb 16 vs Swindon Town (a) 2-1
Att: 16,402 Yorke, Froggatt

6th Round
Mar 8 vs Liverpool (a) 0-1
Att: 29,109

1992/93 SEASON
3rd Round
Jan 2 vs Bristol Rovers (h) 1-1
Att: 27,040 Cox

Replay
Jan 20 vs Bristol Rovers (a) 3-0
Att: 8,880 Saunders 2, Houghton

4th Round
Jan 23 vs Wimbledon (h) 1-1
Att: 21,088 Yorke

Replay
Feb 3 vs Wimbledon (a) 0-0 (aet.)
Att: 8,048 Wimbledon won 6-5 on penalties

1993/94 SEASON
3rd Round
Jan 8 vs Exeter City (a) 1-0
Att: 10,570 Saunders (pen)

4th Round
Jan 29 vs Grimsby Town (a) 2-1
Att: 15,771 Houghton, Yorke

5th Round
Feb 20 vs Bolton Wanderers (a) 0-1
Att: 18,817

1994/95 SEASON
3rd Round
Jan 7 vs Barnsley (a) 2-0
Att: 11,469 Yorke, Saunders

4th Round
Jan 28 vs Manchester City (a) 0-1
Att: 21,177

1995/96 SEASON
3rd Round (at Villa Park)
Jan 6 vs Gravesend & Northfleet 3-0
Att: 26,021   Draper, Milosevic, Johnson
4th Round
Jan 28 vs Sheffield United (a) 1-0
Att: 18,749   Yorke (pen)
5th Round
Feb 17 vs Ipswich Town (a) 3-1
Att: 20,748   Draper, Yorke, Taylor
6th Round
Mar 13 vs Nottingham Forest (a) 1-0
Att: 21,067   Carr
Semi-Final
Mar 31 vs Liverpool (h) 0-3
Att: 39,021

1996/97 SEASON
3rd Round
Jan 14 vs Notts County (a) 0-0
Att: 13,315
Replay
Jan 22 vs Notts County (h) 3-0
Att: 25,006   Yorke 2, Ehiogu
4th Round
Jan 25 vs Derby County (a) 1-3
Att: 17,977   Curcic

1997/98 SEASON
3rd Round
Jan 3 vs Portsmouth (a) 2-2
Att: 16,013   Staunton, Grayson
Replay
Jan 14 vs Portsmouth (h) 1-0
Att: 23,355   Milosevic
4th Round
Jan 24 vs West Bromwich Albion (h) 4-0
Att: 39,372   Grayson, Yorke 2, Collymore
5th Round
Feb 14 vs Coventry City (h) 0-1
Att: 36,979

1998/98 SEASON
3rd Round
Jan 2 vs Hull City (h) 3-0
Att: 39,217   Collymore, Joachim
4th Round
Jan 23 vs Fulham (h) 0-2
Att: 35,260

1999/2000 SEASON
3rd Round
Dec 11 vs Darlington (h) 2-1
Att: 22,101   Carbone, Dublin
4th Round
Jan 8 vs Southampton (h) 1-0
Att: 25,025   Southgate
5th Round
Jan 30 vs Leeds United (h) 3-2
Att: 30,026   Carbone 3
6th Round
Feb 20 vs Everton (a) 2-1
Att: 35,331   Stone, Carbone
Semi-Final (at Wembley)
Apr 2 vs Bolton Wanderers 0-0 (aet)
Att: 62,828   Aston Villa won 4-1 on penalties
FINAL (at Wembley)
May 20 vs Chelsea 0-1
Att: 78,217

2000/2001 SEASON
3rd Round
Jan 7 vs Newcastle United (a) 1-1
Att: 37,862   Stone

Replay
Jan 17 vs Newcastle United (h) 1-0
Att: 25,387   Vassell
4th Round
Jan 27 vs Leicester City (h) 1-2
Att: 26,283   Joachim

2001/2002 SEASON
3rd Round
Jan 6 vs Manchester United (h) 2-3
Att: 38,444   Taylor, Neville P (og)

2002/2003 SEASON
3rd Round
Jan 4 vs Blackburn Rovers (h) 1-4
Att: 23,884   Angel

2003/2004 SEASON
3rd Round
Jan 4 vs Manchester United (h) 1-2
Att: 40,371   Barry

LEAGUE CUP COMPETITION

1974/75 SEASON
2nd Round
Sep 11 vs Everton (h) 1-1
Att: 29,640   Nicholl
Replay
Sep 18 vs Everton (a) 3-0
Att: 24,595   Morgan, Carrodus, Graydon
3rd Round
Oct 9 vs Crewe Alexandra (a) 2-2
Att: 12,290   Morgan, Leonard
Replay
Oct 16 vs Crewe Alexandra (h) 1-0
Att: 24,007   Hamilton
4th Round
Nov 12 vs Hartlepool (a) 1-1
Att: 12,305   Aitken
Replay
Nov 25 vs Hartlepool (h) 6-1
Att: 17,686   Graydon 2 (1 pen), Little B 2, Hamilton 2 (1 pen)
5th Round
Dec 3 vs Colchester United (a) 2-1
Att: 11,871   Little A, Graydon
Semi-Final (1st leg)
Jan 15 vs Chester (a) 2-2
Att: 19,000   McDonald, Graydon
Semi-Final (2nd leg)
Jan 22 vs Chester (h) 3-2 (aggregate 5-4)
Att: 47,732   Leonard 2, Little B
FINAL (at Wembley)
Mar 1 vs Norwich City 1-0
Att: 95,946   Graydon

1975/76 SEASON
2nd Round
Sep 10 vs Oldham Athletic (h) 2-0
Att: 24,138   Leonard, Nicholl
3rd Round
Oct 8 vs Manchester United (h) 1-2
Att: 41,447   Gray

1976/77 SEASON
2nd Round
Sep 1 vs Manchester City (h) 3-0
Att: 35,585   Graydon, Little 2
3rd Round
Sep 21 vs Norwich City (h) 2-1
Att: 31,295   Gray 2

4th Round
Oct 27 vs Wrexham (h) 5-1
Att: 41,428   Nicholl, Little 2, Gray, Carrodus
5th Round
Dec 1 vs Millwall (h) 2-0
Att: 37,147   Nicholl, Little
Semi-Final (1st leg)
Feb 1 vs Queen's Park Rangers (a) 0-0
Att: 28,739
Semi-Final (2nd leg)
Feb 16 vs Q.P.R. (h) 2-2 (aet.) (agg. 2-2)
Att: 48,429   Deehan 2
Semi-Final Replay (at Highbury)
Feb 22 vs Queen's Park Rangers 3-0
Att: 40,438   Little 3
FINAL (at Wembley)
Mar 12 vs Everton 0-0
Att: 96,223
Replay (at Hillsborough)
Mar 16 vs Everton 1-1
Att: 54,840   Kenyon (og)
2nd Replay (at Old Trafford)
Apr 13 vs Everton 3-2 (aet.)
Att: 54,749   Nicholl, Little 2

1977/78 SEASON
2nd Round
Aug 31 vs Exeter City (a) 3-1
Att: 13,768   Gray 3
3rd Round
Oct 26 vs Queen's Park Rangers (h) 1-0
Att: 34,481   Gray (pen)
4th Round
Nov 29 vs Nottingham Forest (a) 2-4
Att: 29,333   Little, Carrodus

1978/79 SEASON
2nd Round
Aug 30 vs Sheffield Wednesday (h) 1-0
Att: 31,152   Shelton
3rd Round
Oct 4 vs Crystal Palace (h) 1-1
Att: 30,690   Little
Replay
Oct 10 vs Crystal Palace (a) 0-0 (aet.)
Att: 33,155
2nd Replay (at Highfield Road)
Oct 16 vs Crystal Palace 3-0
Att: 25,455   Gray 2, Gregory
4th Round
Nov 8 vs Luton Town (h) 0-2
Att: 32,727

1979/80 SEASON
2nd Round (1st leg)
Aug 28 vs Colchester United (a) 2-0
Att: 6,221   Shaw 2
2nd Round (2nd leg)
Sep 5 vs Colchester U (h) 0-2 (aet) (agg 2-2)
Att: 19,473   Aston Villa won 9-8 on penalties
3rd Round
Sep 25 vs Everton (h) 0-0
Att: 22,635
Replay
Oct 9 vs Everton (a) 1-4
Att: 22,088   Swain

1980/81 SEASON
2nd Round (1st leg)
Aug 27 vs Leeds United (h) 1-0
Att: 23,622   Morley

2nd Round (2nd leg)
Sep 3 vs Leeds United (a) 3-1 (agg. 4-1)
Att: 12,236 Shaw 2, Withe

3rd Round
Sep 23 vs Cambridge United (a) 1-2
Att: 7,608 Morley

1981/82 SEASON
2nd Round (1st leg)
Oct 7 vs Wolverhampton Wanderers (h) 3-2
Att: 26,358 Bremner, Morley, Blair

2nd Round (2nd leg)
Oct 27 vs Wolverhampton Wands. (a) 2-1
(aggregate 5-3)
Att: 19,491 Cowans 2 (1 pen)

3rd Round
Nov 11 vs Leicester City (a) 0-0
Att: 19,806

Replay
Nov 25 vs Leicester City (h) 2-0
Att: 23,136 Withe, Cowans (pen)

4th Round
Dec 4 vs Wigan Athletic (a) 2-1
Att: 15,362 Cowans (pen), Withe

5th Round
Jan 20 vs West Bromwich Albion (h) 0-1
Att: 35,197

1982/83 SEASON
2nd Round (1st leg)
Oct 6 vs Notts County (h) 1-2
Att: 16,312 Withe

2nd Round (2nd leg)
Oct 26 vs Notts County (a) 0-1 (agg. 1-3)
Att: 6,921

1983/84 SEASON
2nd Round (1st leg)
Oct 4 vs Portsmouth (a) 2-2
Att: 18,484 Gibson, Evans

2nd Round (2nd leg)
Oct 26 vs Portsmouth (h) 3-2 (agg. 5-4)
Att: 20,898 Evans (pen), Withe, Walters

3rd Round
Nov 9 vs Manchester City (h) 3-0
Att: 23,922 Gibson, Evans, Mortimer

4th Round
Nov 30 vs West Bromwich Albion (a) 2-1
Att: 31,114 Walters, Mortimer

5th Round
Jan 17 vs Norwich City (a) 2-0
Att: 21,568 Shaw, Rideout

Semi-Final (1st leg)
Feb 15 vs Everton (a) 0-2
Att: 40,006

Semi-Final (2nd leg)
Feb 22 vs Everton (h) 1-0 (aggregate 1-2)
Att: 42,426 Rideout

1984/85 SEASON
2nd Round (1st leg)
Sep 24 vs Scunthorpe United (a) 3-2
Att: 6,212 Kerr 2, Gibson

2nd Round (2nd leg)
Oct 10 vs Scunthorpe Utd. (h) 3-1 (agg. 6-3)
Att: 11,421 Cowans, Rideout, Gibson

3rd Round
Oct 30 vs Queen's Park Rangers (a) 0-1
Att: 12,547

1985/86 SEASON
2nd Round (1st leg)
Sep 25 vs Exeter City (h) 4-1
Att: 5,325 Stainrod 4

2nd Round (2nd leg)
Oct 9 vs Exeter City (h) 8-1 (agg. 12-2)
*Att: 7,678 Williams 2, Ormsby 2, Birch,
Stainrod, Gray 2*

3rd Round
Oct 30 vs Leeds United (a) 3-0
Att: 15,444 Stainrod 2, Walters

4th Round
Nov 20 vs West Bromwich Albion (h) 2-2
Att: 20,204 Stainrod, Evans (pen)

Replay
Nov 27 vs West Bromwich Albion (a) 2-1
Att: 18,629 Hodge, Walters

5th Round
Jan 22 vs Arsenal (h) 1-1
Att: 26,093 Glover

Replay
Feb 4 vs Arsenal (a) 2-1
Att: 33,091 Birch, Evans

Semi-Final (1st leg)
Mar 4 vs Oxford United (h) 2-2
Att: 23,098 Birch, Stainrod

Semi-Final (2nd leg)
Mar 12 vs Oxford United (a) 1-2 (agg. 3-4)
Att: 13,989 Walters

1986/87 SEASON
2nd Round (1st leg)
Sep 24 vs Reading (a) 1-1
Att: 9,363 Hodge

2nd Round (2nd leg)
Oct 8 vs Reading (h) 4-1 (aggregate 5-2)
Att: 12,484 Gray 2, Hodge, Walters

3rd Round
Oct 29 vs Derby County (a) 1-1
Att: 19,374 Daley

Replay
Nov 4 vs Derby County (h) 2-1
Att: 19,477 Thompson, Birch

4th Round
Nov 18 vs Southampton (a) 1-2
Att: 13,402 Evans

1987/88 SEASON
2nd Round (1st leg)
Sep 23 vs Middlesbrough (a) 1-0
Att: 11,424 Aspinall

2nd Round (2nd leg)
Oct 7 vs Middlesbrough (h) 1-0 (agg. 2-0)
Att: 11,702 Birch

3rd Round
Oct 28 vs Tottenham Hotspur (h) 2-1
Att: 29,114 McInally, Aspinall

4th Round
Nov 18 vs Sheffield Wednesday (h) 1-2
Att: 25,302 Thompson

1988/89 SEASON
2nd Round (1st leg)
Sep 27 vs Birmingham City (a) 2-0
Att: 21,177 Gage, Gray A

2nd Round (2nd leg)
Oct 12 vs Birmingham C. (h) 5-0 (agg. 7-0)
*Att: 19,753 Mountfield, Gage 2, Olney,
Daley*

3rd Round
Nov 2 vs Millwall (h) 3-1
Att: 17,648 McInally 2, Platt

4th Round
Nov 30 vs Ipswich Town (h) 6-2
Att: 16,284 McInally 2, Platt 4

5th Round
Jan 18 vs West Ham United (a) 1-2
Att: 30,110 Platt

1989/90 SEASON
2nd Round (1st leg)
Sep 20 vs Wolverhampton Wands. (h) 2-1
Att: 27,400 Platt, Gray

2nd Round (2nd leg)
Oct 4 vs Wolv'hampton W. (a) 1-1 (agg 3-2)
Att: 22,754 Mountfield

3rd Round
Oct 25 vs West Ham United (h) 0-0
Att: 20,898

Replay
Nov 8 vs West Ham United (a) 0-1
Att: 23,833

1990/91 SEASON
2nd Round (1st leg)
Sep 26 vs Barnsley (h) 1-0
Att: 14,471 Platt

2nd Round (2nd leg)
Oct 9 vs Barnsley (a) 1-0
Att: 13,924 Daley

3rd Round
Oct 31 vs Millwall (h) 2-0
Att: 15,117 Cascarino, Platt (pen)

4th Round
Nov 28 vs Middlesbrough (h) 3-2
Att: 17,317 Ormondroyd, Daley, Platt (pen)

5th Round
Jan 16 vs Leeds United (a) 1-2
Att: 28,176 Ormondroyd

1991/92 SEASON
2nd Round (1st leg)
Sep 25 vs Grimsby Town (a) 0-0
Att: 13,835

2nd Round (2nd leg)
Oct 9 vs Grimsby Town (h) 1-1 (agg. 1-1)
Att: 15,338 Teale
Grimsby Town won on away goals

1992/93 SEASON
2nd Round (1st leg)
Sep 23 vs Oxford United (a) 2-1
Att: 8,837 McGrath, Teale

2nd Round (2nd leg)
Oct 7 vs Oxford United (h) 2-1 (agg. 4-2)
Att: 19,808 Atkinson, Richardson

3rd Round
Oct 28 vs Manchester United (h) 1-0
Att: 35,964 Saunders

4th Round
Dec 2 vs Ipswich Town (h) 2-2
Att: 21,545 Atkinson, Saunders

Replay
Dec 15 vs Ipswich Town (a) 0-1
Att: 19,196

1993/94 SEASON
2nd Round (1st leg)
Sep 21 vs Birmingham City (a) 1-0
Att: 27,815 Richardson

2nd Round (2nd leg)
Oct 6 vs Birmingham City (h) 1-0 (agg. 2-0)
Att: 35,856 Saunders

3rd Round
Oct 26 vs Sunderland (a) 4-1
*Att: 23,692 Atkinson 2, Richardson,
Houghton*

4th Round
Nov 30 vs Arsenal (a) 1-0
Att: 26,453   Atkinson

5th Round
Jan 12 vs Tottenham Hotspur (a) 2-1
Att: 31,408   Houghton, Barrett

Semi-Final (1st leg)
Feb 16 vs Tranmere Rovers (a) 1-3
Att: 17,140   Atkinson

Semi-Final (2nd leg)
Feb 27 vs Tranmere R (h) 3-1 (aet) (agg 4-4)
Att: 40,593   Saunders, Teale, Atkinson
Aston Villa won 5-4 on penalties

FINAL (at Wembley)
Mar 27 vs Manchester United 3-1
Att: 77,231   Atkinson, Saunders 2 (1 pen)

1994/95 SEASON
2nd Round (1st leg)
Sep 21 vs Wigan Athletic (h) 5-0
Att: 12,433   Yorke, Atkinson 2, Saunders,
Lamptey

2nd Round (2nd leg)
Oct 5 vs Wigan Athletic (a) 3-0 (agg. 8-0)
Att: 2,633   Lamptey 2, Whittingham

3rd Round
Oct 26 vs Middlesbrough (h) 1-0
Att: 19,254   Townsend

4th Round
Nov 30 vs Crystal Palace (a) 1-4
Att: 12,653   Atkinson

1995/96 SEASON
2nd Round (1st leg)
Sep 20 vs Peterborough United (h) 6-0
Att: 19,602   Draper, Yorke 2 (2 pens),
Johnson, Heald (og), Southgate

2nd Round (2nd leg)
Oct 3 vs Peterborough U (a) 1-1 (agg. 7-1)
Att: 5,745   Staunton

3rd Round
Oct 25 vs Stockport County (h) 2-0
Att: 17,679   Ehiogu, Yorke

4th Round
Nov 29 vs Queen's Park Rangers (h) 1-0
Att: 24,951   Townsend

5th Round
Jan 10 vs Wolverhampton Wands. (h) 1-0
Att: 39,277   Johnson

Semi-Final (1st leg)
Feb 14 vs Arsenal (a) 2-2
Att: 37,562   Yorke 2

Semi-Final (2nd leg)
Feb 21 vs Arsenal (h) 0-0 (aet)
Att: 39,334   Aston Villa won on away goals

FINAL (at Wembley)
Mar 24 vs Leeds United 3-0
Att: 77,056   Milosevic, Taylor, Yorke

1996/97 SEASON
3rd Round
Oct 23 vs Leeds United (a) 2-1
Att: 15,803   Taylor, Yorke (pen)

4th Round
Nov 26 vs Wimbledon (h) 0-1
Att: 7,573

1997/98 SEASON
3rd Round
Oct 15 vs West Ham (a) 0-3
Att: 20,360

1998/99 SEASON
3rd Round
Oct 28 vs Chelsea (a) 1-4
Att: 26,790   Draper

1999/2000 SEASON
2nd Round (1st leg)
Sep 14 vs Chester City (a) 1-0
Att: 4,364   Hendrie

2nd Round (2nd leg)
Sep 21 vs Chester City (h) 5-0 (agg. 6-0)
Att: 22,613   Boateng, Taylor, Hendrie 2,
Thompson

3rd Round
Oct 13 vs Manchester United (h) 3-0
Att: 33,815   Joachim, Taylor, Stone

4th Round
Dec 1 vs Southampton (h) 4-0
Att: 17,608   Watson, Joachim, Dublin 2

5th Round
*Dec 15 vs West Ham United (a) 2-2 (aet)
West Ham United won 5-4 on penalties but the
match was ordered to be replayed as West Ham
had fielded an ineligible player.

Replay
Jan 11 vs West Ham United (a) 3-1 (aet)
Att: 25,592   Taylor 2, Joachim

Semi-Final (1st leg)
Jan 25 vs Leicester City (h) 0-0
Att: 28,037

Semi-Final (2nd leg)
Feb 2 vs Leicester City (a) 0-1 (agg. 0-1)
Att: 21,843

2000/2001 SEASON
3rd Round
Nov 1 vs Manchester City (h) 0-1
Att: 24,138

2001/2002 SEASON
3rd Round
Oct 10 vs Reading (h) 1-0
Att: 23,431   Dublin

4th Round
Nov 28 vs Sheffield Wednesday (h) 0-1
Att: 26,526

2002/2003 SEASON
2nd Round
Oct 2 vs Luton Town (h) 3-0
Att: 20,833   De la Cruz, Dublin 2

3rd Round
Nov 6 vs Oxford United (a) 3-0
Att: 12,177   Taylor, Barry, Dublin

4th Round
Dec 4 vs Preston North End (h) 5-0
Att: 23,042   Vassell 2, Dublin, Angel,
Hitzlsperger

5th Round
Dec 18 vs Liverpool (h) 3-4
Att: 38,530   Vassell (pen), Hitzlsperger,
Henchoz (og)

2003/2004 SEASON
2nd Round
Sep 23 vs Wycombe Wanderers (a) 5-0
Att: 6,072   Whittingham, Angel 3, Vassell

3rd Round
Oct 29 vs Leicester City (h) 1-0
Att: 26,729   Hitzlsperger

4th Round
Dec 3 vs Crystal Palace (h) 3-0
Att: 24,258   Angel 2, McCann

5th Round
Dec 17 vs Chelsea (h) 2-1
Att: 30,414   Angel, McCann

Semi-Final (1st leg)
Jan 21 vs Bolton Wanderers (a) 2-5
Att: 16,302   Angel 2

Semi-Final (2nd leg)
Jan 27 vs Bolton Wands. (h) 2-0 (agg. 4-5)
Att: 36,883   Hitzlsperger, Samuel

EUROPEAN CHAMPIONS CUP
1981/82 SEASON
1st Round (1st leg)
Sep 16 vs Valur Reykjavik (h) 5-0
Att: 20,481   Morley, Withe 2, Donovan 2

1st Round (2nd leg)
Sep 30 vs Valur Reyjavik (a) 2-0 (agg. 7-0)
Att: 3,500   Shaw 2

2nd Round (1st leg)
Oct 21 vs Dynamo Berlin (a) 2-1
Att: 31,000   Morley 2

2nd Round (2nd leg)
Nov 4 vs Dynamo Berlin (h) 0-1 (agg. 2-2)
Att: 28,175   Aston Villa won on Away Goals

Quarter-Final (1st leg)
Mar 3 vs Dynamo Kiev (a) 0-0
Att: 36,000

Quarter-Final (2nd leg)
Mar 17 vs Dynamo Kiev (h) 2-0 (agg. 2-0)
Att: 38,579   Shaw, McNaught

Semi-Final (1st leg)
Apr 7 vs Anderlecht (h) 1-0
Att: 38,539   Morley

Semi-Final (2nd leg)
Apr 21 vs Anderlecht (a) 0-0 (agg. 1-0)
Att: 28,000

FINAL
May 26 vs Bayern Munich 1-0
Att: 46,000   Withe

1982/83 SEASON
1st Round (1st leg)
Sep 15 vs Besiktas (h) 3-1
Att: (Behind closed doors)   Withe, Morley,
Mortimer

1st Round (2nd leg)
Sep 29 vs Besiktas (a) 0-0 (aggregate 3-1)
Att: 45,000

2nd Round (1st leg)
Oct 20 vs Dynamo Bucharest (a) 2-0
Att: 70,000   Shaw 2

2nd Round (2nd leg)
Nov 3 vs Dyn. Bucharest (h) 4-2 (agg. 6-2)
Att: 22,244   Shaw 3, Walters

Quarter-Final (1st leg)
Mar 2 vs Juventus (h) 1-2
Att: 45,531   Cowans

Quarter-Final (2nd leg)
Mar 16 vs Juventus (a) 1-3 (aggregate 2-5)
Att: 66,000   Withe

UEFA CUP COMPETITION
1975/76 SEASON
1st Round (1st leg)
Sep 17 vs Antwerp (a) 1-4
Att: 21,000   Graydon

1st Round (2nd leg)
Oct 1 vs Antwerp (h) 0-1 (aggregate 1-5)
Att: 31,513

1977/78 SEASON
1st Round (1st leg)
Sep 14 vs Fenerbahce (h) 4-0
Att: 30,351 Gray, Deehan 2, Little

1st Round (2nd leg)
Sep 28 vs Fenerbahce (a) 2-0 (agg. 6-0)
Att: 25,000

2nd Round (1st leg)
Oct 19 vs Gornik Zabrze (h) 2-0
Att: 34,138 McNaught 2

2nd Round (2nd leg)
Nov 2 vs Gornik Zabrze (a) 1-1 (agg. 3-1)
Att: 15,000 Gray

3rd Round (1st leg)
Nov 23 vs Athletic Bilbao (h) 2-0
Att: 32,973 Iribar (og), Deehan

3rd Round (2nd leg)
Dec 7 vs Athletic Bilbao (a) 1-1 (agg. 3-1)
Att: 39,000 Mortimer

Quarter-Final (1st leg)
Mar 1 vs Barcelona (h) 2-2
Att: 49,619 McNaught, Deehan

Quarter-Final (2nd leg)
Mar 15 vs Barcelona (a) 1-2 (agg. 3-4)
Att: 90,000 Little

1983/84 SEASON
1st Round (1st leg)
Sep 14 vs Vitoria Guimaraes (a) 0-1
Att: 28,750

1st Round (2nd leg)
Sep 28 vs Vit. Guimaraes (h) 5-0 (agg. 5-1)
Att: 23,732 Withe 3, Ormsby, Gibson

2nd Round (1st leg)
Oct 19 vs Spartak Moscow (a) 2-2
Att: 50,400 Gibson, Walters

2nd Round (2nd leg)
Nov 2 vs Spartak Moscow (h) 1-2 (agg 3-4)
Att: 29,511 Withe

1990/91 SEASON
1st Round (1st leg)
Sep 19 vs Banik Ostrava (h) 3-1
Att: 27,317 Platt, Mountfield, Olney

1st Round (2nd leg)
Oct 3 vs Banik Ostrava (a) 2-1 (agg. 5-2)
Att: 20,000 Mountfield, Stas (og)

2nd Round (1st leg)
Oct 24 vs Internazionale (h) 2-0
Att: 36,461 Nielsen, Platt

2nd Round (2nd leg)
Nov 7 vs Internazionale (a) 0-3 (agg. 2-3)
Att: 80,000

1993/94 SEASON
1st Round (1st leg)
Sep 15 vs Slovan Bratislava (a) 0-0
Att: 10,886

1st Round (2nd leg)
Sep 29 vs Slovan Bratislava (h) 2-1
(aggregate 2-1)
Att: 24,461 Atkinson, Townsend

2nd Round (1st leg)
Oct 19 vs La Coruna (a) 1-1
Att: 26,800 Saunders

2nd Round (2nd leg)
Nov 3 vs La Coruna (h) 0-1 (aggregate 1-2)
Att: 26,737

1994/95 SEASON
1st Round (1st leg)
Sep 15 vs Inter Milan (a) 0-1
Att: 22,639

1st Round (2nd leg)
Sep 29 vs Inter Milan (h) 1-0 (aet)(agg 1-1)
Att: 30,533 Houghton
Aston Villa won 4-2 on penalties

2nd Round (1st leg)
Oct 18 vs Trabzonspor (a) 0-1
Att: 27,500

2nd Round (2nd leg)
Nov 1 vs Trabzonspor (h) 2-1 (aet) (agg 2-2)
Att: 23,858 Atkinson, Ehiogu
Trabzonspor won on Away Goals

1996/97 SEASON
1st Round (1st leg)
Sep 10 vs Helsingborg (h) 1-1
Att: 25,818 Johnson

1st Round (2nd leg)
Sep 24 vs Helsingborg (a) 0-0 (agg 1-1)
Att: 16,000 Helsingborg won on Away Goals

1997/98 SEASON
1st Round (1st leg)
Sep 16 vs Bordeaux (a) 0-0
Att: 16,800

1st Round (2nd leg)
Sep 30 vs Bordeaux (h) 1-0 (aggregate 1-0)
Att: 33,072 Milosevic

2nd Round (1st leg)
Oct 21 vs Athletic Bilbao (a) 0-0
Att: 39,000

2nd Round (2nd leg)
Nov 4 vs Athletic Bilbao (h) 2-1 (agg. 2-1)
Att: 35,915 Taylor, Yorke

3rd Round (1st leg)
Nov 25 vs Steaua (a) 1-2
Att: 24,000 Yorke

3rd Round (2nd leg)
Dec 9 vs Steaua (h) 2-0 (aggregate 3-2)
Att: 35,102 Milosevic, Taylor

Quarter-Final (1st leg)
Mar 3 vs Atletico Madrid (a) 0-1
Att: 51,000

Quarter-Final (2nd leg)
Mar 17 vs Atletico Madrid (h) 2-1 (agg. 2-2)
Att: 39,163 Taylor, Collymore
Atletico Madrid won on Away Goals

1998/99 SEASON
1st Round (1st leg)
Sep 15 vs Stromsgodset (h) 3-2
Att: 28,893 Charles, Vassell 2

1st Round (2nd leg)
Sep 29 vs Stromsgodset (a) 3-0 (agg. 6-2)
Att: 4,835 Collymore 3

2nd Round (1st leg)
Oct 20 vs Celta Vigo (a) 1-0
Att: 25,000 Joachim

2nd Round (2nd leg)
Nov 3 vs Celta Vigo (h) 1-3 (aggregate 2-3)
Att: 29,910 Collymore (pen)

2001/2002 SEASON
1st Round (1st leg)
Sep 20 vs Varteks (h) 2-3
Att: 27,132 Angel 2

1st Round (2nd leg)
Sep 27 vs Varteks (a) 1-0 (aggregate 3-3)
Att: 12,100 Hadji
Varteks won on the away goals rule

Supporters' Guides & Other Titles

This top-selling series has been published annually since 1982 and contains 2003/2004 Season's results and tables, Directions, Photographs, Phone numbers, Parking information, Admission details, Disabled information and much more.

THE SUPPORTERS' GUIDE TO PREMIER & FOOTBALL LEAGUE CLUBS 2005

The 21st edition featuring all Premiership and Football League clubs. *Price £6.99*

THE SUPPORTERS' GUIDE TO NON-LEAGUE FOOTBALL 2005 – STEP 1 & STEP 2 CLUBS

Following the reorganisation of Non-League Football this 13th edition covers all 66 Step 1 & Step 2 clubs – effectively the Football Conference and it's feeder Leagues. *Price £6.99*

THE SUPPORTERS' GUIDE TO NON-LEAGUE FOOTBALL 2005 – STEP 3 CLUBS

Following the reorganisation of Non-League Football the 1st edition of this book features all 66 clubs which feed into the Football Conference. *Price £6.99*

THE SUPPORTERS' GUIDE TO SCOTTISH FOOTBALL 2005

The 13th edition featuring all Scottish Premier League, Scottish League and Highland League clubs. *Price £6.99*

THE SUPPORTERS' GUIDE TO WELSH FOOTBALL GROUNDS 2005

The 9th edition featuring all League of Wales, Cymru Alliance & Welsh Football League Clubs + results, tables & much more. *Price £6.99*

FOOTBALL LEAGUE TABLES 1888-2004

The 7th edition contains every Football League, Premier League, Scottish League and Scottish Premier League Final Table from 1888-2004 together with Cup Final Information. *Price £9.99*

NON-LEAGUE FOOTBALL TABLES 1889-2004

The 3rd edition contains final tables for the Conference, it's 3 feeder Leagues and 4 Northern Leagues in England (which were not included in previous editions). *Price £9.95*

These books are available UK & Surface post free from –

Soccer Books Limited (Dept. SBL)
72 St. Peter's Avenue
Cleethorpes
N.E. Lincolnshire
DN35 8HU

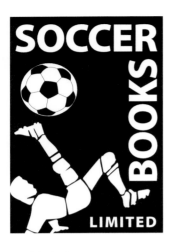

SOCCER BOOKS LIMITED

72 ST. PETERS AVENUE (Dept. SBL)
CLEETHORPES
N.E. LINCOLNSHIRE
DN35 8HU
ENGLAND

Tel. 01472 696226   Fax 01472 698546

Web site www.soccer-books.co.uk
e-mail info@soccer-books.co.uk

Established in 1982, Soccer Books Limited has the biggest range of English-Language soccer books and videos available. We are now expanding our stocks even further to include many more titles including German, French, Spanish and Italian-language books.

With over 100,000 satisfied customers already, we supply books to virtually every country in the world but have maintained the friendliness and accessibility associated with a small family-run business. The range of titles we sell includes:

YEARBOOKS – All major yearbooks including Sky Sports/Rothmans (many editions), Calcios, Supporters' Guides, Playfair Annuals, North & Latin American Guides (all editions), African Guides, Non-League Directories.

CLUB HISTORIES – Complete Statistical Records, Official Histories, 25 Year Records, Definitive Histories plus many more.

WORLD FOOTBALL – World Cup books, Complete Results & Line-ups Series, European Championships History, International Statistical Histories and much more.

BIOGRAPHIES & WHO'S WHOS – of Managers and Players plus Who's Whos etc.

ENCYCLOPEDIAS & GENERAL TITLES – Books on Stadia, Hooligan studies, Histories and dozens of others.

DVDs & VIDEOS – Season's highlights, histories, big games, World Cup, player profiles, F.A. Cup Finals with many more titles becoming available all the time.

For a current printed listing of a range of our titles, please contact us using the information at the top of the page.

Our web site offers a secure ordering system for credit/debit card holders and lists our range of over 1,100 new books, hundreds of videos and an ever increasing number of DVDs.